SCIENTIFIC STUDIES OF READING

Volume 6, Number 3   2002

SPECIAL ISSUE
Reading Development in Adults
Richard L. Venezky and John P. Sabatini, *Guest Editors*

T0347281

ANNOUNCEMENT

Frank Manis at the University of Southern California is now Editor Elect of *Scientific Studies of Reading*. New submissions should be sent to him at Psychology Department, University of Southern California, Los Angeles CA 90089.

SCIENTIFIC STUDIES OF READING, 6(3), 217–220
Copyright © 2002, Lawrence Erlbaum Associates, Inc.

Introduction to This Special Issue: Reading Development in Adults

Richard L. Venezky
School of Education
University of Delaware

John P. Sabatini
National Center on Adult Literacy
University of Pennsylvania

A panel of literacy experts from various disciplines, convened recently to advise various federal agencies on research priorities in adult and family literacy, concluded that "much additional research is needed on both adult and family literacy" (National Institute of Child Health and Human Development [NICHD], 2001). Although the top priority for the panel was research on effective instructional methods, it also called for further research on "basic reading processes in adult learners" (NICHD, 2001). Compared to basic process research on children, which enjoys a 100-year history, a range of standardized measures in several different languages, and a deep research literature (however mixed the quality might be), basic research on the reading processes of low-literacy adults is impoverished. Although the earliest experimental studies in psychology, performed in Wundt's laboratory in Leipzig in the 1880s, were on adult reading processes, the primary interest then was individual differences in the speed of mental events, and the participants were almost always fully literate adults. Interest in the basic perceptual and cognitive processes of adults learning to read is a phenomenon of the last 3 decades, with few sustained research programs, few standardized measures, and limited agreement on how to define experimental populations.

Requests for reprints should be sent to Richard L. Venezky, University of Delaware, Willard Hall, Newark, DE 19716. E-mail: venezky@dewey.udel.edu

This issue of *Scientific Studies of Reading* is a snapshot of current research in this area, showing many of the issues encountered, the methods employed, and the limitations faced. All four studies involve experimental or quasi-experimental studies; however, all are based on participants recruited from adult literacy programs. According to some estimates, this population represents less than 10% of those adults who need better literacy skills (Venezky & Wagner, 1996). However inexact this figure might be for the U.S. adult population, it nevertheless brings attention to the difficulties of recruiting a random sample of low-literacy adults. Implementing longitudinal studies of instruction is even more problematic, due to a high dropout rate from adult literacy programs (Development Associates, 1994). However, the one instructional study reported here (Durgunoğlu & Öney), done in Turkey, did not suffer from this problem.

A second problem in selecting study populations is that a relatively high percentage of low-literacy adults in the United States had or still have learning disabilities, yet little agreement exists on how to define and measure these for an adult population (Johnson & Blalock, 1987). In one study reported here (Sabatini), for example, 38% of the participants self-reported learning problems. It is difficult, therefore, to compare results of different studies, even when various reading abilities are equated. The expert panel mentioned previously noted this issue, stating that "there is a pressing need for the development of both screening and diagnostic assessment tools for the identification of adults with reading or other learning disabilities that might hinder the development of reading and writing" (NICHD, 2001).

The studies presented in this issue focus on processing differences across native and nonnative English speakers (Davidson & Strucker), children and adults (Greenberg, Ehri, & Perin; Durgunoğlu & Öney), adults before and after instruction (Durgunoğlu & Öney), and adults at different levels of reading ability (Sabatini). They question whether adult literacy development follows the same developmental course as that for children; what role speed processing plays in reading performance; how reading abilities gained in a first language impact processing in a second language; and how linguistic ability, language characteristics, and writing system features impact learning to read and write.

Greenberg et al. matched normally developing children and reading grade equivalent adult learners (grade equivalents 3–5) on gender, race, and residential area and examined their word recognition errors. The results, coupled with measures of phonological processing and decoding, show that adults tend to use more visual/orthographic strategies when encountering word recognition problems, whereas children reading at the same grade equivalent use decoding and other phonetic strategies for both word recognition and spelling. Durgunoğlu and Öney tested a sample of women in a functional adult literacy program before and after 90 hr of literacy instruction on a number of basic processing skills and compared the results to data obtained in earlier studies from children learning to read. Although they conclude that, for Turkish, the literacy development processes are the same for children and adults, they found that phonological awareness functioned differently as a predictor of reading ability after the 1st year (or 90-hr course) for the two populations. They also found, in comparing their results to those found for English-speaking children in the United States, that the roles played by letter recognition, phonological awareness, and listening comprehension are language specific.

Sabatini tested a range of adult readers, including those from adult literacy programs as well as those enrolled in college programs, on both speed and accuracy of basic reading and comprehension processes. Whereas the high-ability group showed both high speed and high accuracy, with word and pseudoword naming rates faster than rates for naming line drawings, the low-ability groups showed significantly slower naming rates and processing accuracy, with rates for naming words and pseudowords significantly slower than rates for naming line drawings. This double-deficit pattern, wherein both phonological processing and speed of word/pseudoword processing are deficient, is characteristic of many low-literacy adults and may result in reduced benefits from exposure to print.

Davidson and Strucker compared the word substitution errors of native English speakers and nonnative English speakers, all drawn from adult basic education and adult secondary education programs, with grade equivalent reading abilities in the range of 4 to 6. The group of native speakers averaged almost 2.5 times as many real-word substitutions as the nonnative speakers group, whereas the latter averaged almost 2.4 times as many phonetically plausible errors as the former even though their decoding scores were identical. These results demonstrate that identical decoding scores on a standardized measure do not guarantee identical uses of decoding. Important differences were also found for skill profiles and for basic processing within the nonnative speakers of English group according to length of time in the United States.

Together these studies do not make any major breakthroughs or overturn any cherished beliefs. But they do illuminate many of the gray areas of adult basic processing, particularly for adults in basic skills programs, and they present many of the complexities of studying low-literacy adults: the high percentages with learning disabilities, the differences across native and nonnative English speakers and within classes of the latter, the different processing abilities of adults and children matched for reading ability, the impacts of language and orthography on reading strategies, and the importance of measuring speed as well as accuracy in studying basic processing. As the study of low-literacy adults matures, we can expect to see stronger theoretical foundations, more agreement on definitions and measurement techniques, and better access to those low-literacy adults who are unwilling or unable to attend adult literacy classes. The studies in this issue of *SSR*, among others, are an indication that scientific programs exist and are at work on key issues.

ACKNOWLEDGMENTS

As a final note, we thank the reviewers of this issue for their timely and thoughtful work: Jane Ashby, James Booth, Joanne Carlisle, Anne Fowler, Noel Gregg, John Krudnenier, Connie Varnhagen, and Maryanne Wolf.

REFERENCES

Davidson, R. K., & Strucker, J. (2002). Patterns of word-recognition errors among adult basic education native and nonnative speakers of English. *Scientific Studies of Reading, 6,* 299–316.

Development Associates, Inc. (1994). *National evaluation of adult education programs: Patterns and predictors of client attendance.* Washington, DC: U.S. Department of Education.

Durgunoğlu, A. Y., & Öney, B. (2002). Phonological awareness in literacy acquisition: It's not only for children. *Scientific Studies of Reading, 6,* 245–266.

Greenberg, D., Ehri, L. C., & Perin, D. (2002). Do adult literacy students make the same word-reading and spelling errors as children matched for word-reading age? *Scientific Studies of Reading, 6,* 221–243.

Johnson, D. J., & Blalock, J. W. (1987). *Adults with learning disabilities.* New York: Harcourt Brace.

National Institute of Child Health and Human Development. (2001). *Adult and family literacy: Current research and future directions—A workshop summary* (Informal summary report). Bethesda, MD: Author. Retrieved November 29, 2001, from http://www.nichd.nih.gov/crmc_cdb/AFL_workshop.htm

Sabatini, J. (2002). Efficiency in word reading of adults: Ability group comparisons. *Scientific Studies of Reading, 6,* 267–298.

Venezky, R. L., & Wagner, D. A. (1996). Supply and demand for adult literacy instruction. *Adult Education Quarterly, 46,* 197–208.

SCIENTIFIC STUDIES OF READING, 6(3), 221–243
Copyright © 2002, Lawrence Erlbaum Associates, Inc.

Do Adult Literacy Students Make the Same Word-Reading and Spelling Errors as Children Matched for Word-Reading Age?

Daphne Greenberg

Georgia State University

Linnea C. Ehri

Graduate Center, City University of New York

Dolores Perin

Teachers College, Columbia University

In this study, an analysis was undertaken of the word-reading and spelling error patterns of 72 adult literacy students and 72 normally developing child readers who read words at the same grade-equivalent levels. Their utilization of orthographic and phonological strategies to read sight words, to decode nonwords, to spell words, and to detect rhyming words was analyzed. Results indicated that when encountering difficulties adults were less likely than children to use phonological strategies and were more likely than children to rely on visual or orthographic processes. Adults' misreadings were more often real words whereas children's misreadings revealed decoding mistakes. Adults' spellings were more often prephonetic or nonphonetic than children's spellings. Adults had difficulty detecting rhyming pairs of words unless the words had similar spellings. Findings are consistent with the view that adults' poor graphophonemic and decoding skills contribute to their difficulties reading and spelling words.

Requests for reprints should be sent to Daphne Greenberg, Center for the Study of Adult Literacy, Georgia State University, University Plaza, Atlanta, GA 30303–3083.

The field of adult literacy suffers from a paucity of thorough and methodologically sound studies. Researchers have not investigated the learning processes of adults nearly as extensively as those of children and adolescents. As a result, very little is known about the word-reading processes of low-literate adults. Although the National Adult Literacy Survey (Kirsch, Jungeblut, Jenkins, & Kolstad, 1993) identified adults who had difficulty performing everyday tasks, the survey focused on comprehension and functional literacy tasks and therefore may have overestimated the word-reading skills of low-literate adults (Perfetti & Marron, 1995). Additionally, the survey did not explore the underlying word-reading deficits that would help explain the nature of low-reading adults' weaknesses (Snow & Strucker, 2000).

As part of a program of research to compare the word-reading skills of low-literate adults to younger, normally developing readers, this study analyzed in more detail data collected in an earlier study (Greenberg, Ehri, & Perin, 1997). In the previous work, adult literacy students and elementary students were matched for grade-equivalent levels in word reading. Students were reading at third-, fourth-, and fifth-grade-equivalent levels as assessed by the Word Identification subtest of the Woodcock Reading Mastery Test–Revised (Woodcock, 1987). Several tasks were administered to participants to assess the processes that they use to read words, including sounding out and blending nonwords to pronounce them, segmenting and deleting phonemes in words, reading irregularly spelled words by sight, and detecting frequent and infrequent orthographic sequences in words. Findings indicated that adults showed strength in some of the orthographic tasks but severe weakness in the phonological tasks when compared to the normally developing children.

Previous research has indicated that adult literacy students possess relative strength in the area of orthographic knowledge but serious deficits in the phonological domain (e.g., Bruck, 1993; Castro-Caldas, Petersson, Reis, Stone-Elander, & Ingvar, 1998; Fawcett & Nicholson, 1995; Gottesman, Bennett, Nathan, & Kelly, 1996; Lindamood, Bell, & Lindamood, 1992). The current study used error analysis to investigate further the phonological and orthographic processing differences that were observed by Greenberg et al. (1997). Error patterns provide rich information about the course of development in normally developing readers as well as students who are struggling to make progress (Bruck, 1993; Liberman, Rubin, Duques, & Carlisle, 1985; Perin, 1998; Worthy & Viise, 1996). Analysis of errors can provide qualitative information to elucidate the strategies or knowledge sources that underlie group differences in literacy performance. In the area of spelling, for example, errors have been described as "a visible record of disordered language processing" (Moats, 1993, p. 174). Observation of young children's errors was the starting point for the development of several major theories of literacy acquisition (Ehri, 1986; Frith, 1985; Marsh, Friedman, Welch, & Desberg, 1981; see Snowling, 2000). Acquired and developmental dyslexias in both children and adults have been diagnosed based on error patterns (Goldsmith-Phillips, 1994; Iribarren, Jarema, & Lecours, 1999; Temple & Marshall, 1983). Error patterns are also important for planning instructional interventions (Sawyer, Wade, & Kim, 1999; Shaughnessy, 1977).

Responses to tasks that differed in terms of the degree of involvement of phonological or orthographic processes were analyzed. Of interest was whether the differences favoring children on the more phonological tasks and adults on the more orthographic tasks were mainly quantitative, with the groups displaying different accuracy levels but similar types of errors, or whether the differences were qualitative, with the groups showing differences in the types of errors produced. Results showing only quantitative differences would suggest that the adults were utilizing the same cognitive-linguistic processes as children to read and spell words. This was the conclusion reached by Greenberg et al. (1997) based on a regression analysis showing that the same processes explained variance in the word-reading task for the two groups. However, we assumed that analysis of their errors could provide additional evidence for different cognitive-linguistic processes or strategies used by the two groups, including compensatory strategies. In general, we hypothesized that regardless of whether the tasks highlighted orthographic or phonological involvement, the error analyses would indicate that the adults and children produced different types of errors, with the adults favoring a more orthographic strategy and the children favoring a more phonological strategy when reading and spelling words.

The orthographic task that was chosen was Adams' and Huggins' (1985) sight word reading consisting of 50 irregularly spelled words such as *yacht* and *bouquet*. This task is considered to highlight orthographic processes because it requires remembering letter sequences associated with individual words. The words are atypically spelled and cannot be read correctly by the application of spelling–sound correspondence rules. Greenberg et al. (1997) found that adults read significantly more sight words than children did at all word-reading grade levels.

When individuals are presented with sight words that are graduated in difficulty, Adams and Huggins (1985) found that they read words easily until they reach a point where the words are less familiar and not fully represented in their sight vocabularies. They then begin making errors. When they come across words they do not know, they may phonologically recode the words or they may misread the words as other real words. Phonological recoding is evident if they pronounce the words as they are spelled, for example, *tongue* as /tongyu/ (long *u*). Because we found that adults were poorer at decoding nonwords than children, we expected that few of their errors would show phonological recoding strategies. Rather we expected them to guess by saying other familiar words. We also hypothesized that when adults and children misread sight words as other real words, the two groups would produce different real-word substitutions because they are exposed daily to different types of words. Whereas normally developing children see a great many school words, adults see more words associated with the adult commercial environment.

The phonological task that was chosen was the Word Attack subtest of the Woodcock Reading Mastery Test–Revised (Woodcock, 1987) consisting of 45 pseudowords. This task is considered to highlight phonological involvement because it requires individuals to decode items that can be pronounced but have no meaning in English and therefore cannot be retrieved as whole words from an internal lexicon. The phonological focus of this task comes from the need to assemble and hold in memory phonemes derived from graphemes and then blend these to form pronunciations. Greenberg et al. (1997) found that children correctly read significantly more nonsense words than adults did at all word-reading grade levels. It was hypothesized that the adults, because of their poor phonological skills, would not utilize phonological strategies to the same degree as the children but rather would resort to reading nonwords as real words, utilizing a more orthographic strategy.

The relative orthographic and phonological involvement of different tasks can be depicted as a continuum. As already indicated, some tasks such as sight word reading are considered to be more orthographic, whereas tasks such as reading nonwords are considered to be more phonological. However, other tasks can be said to involve both types of processes, and, in this study, spelling production and rhyme detection tasks were chosen to represent these types of tasks.

Spelling production requires both orthographic and phonological knowledge to determine how phonemes in words should be visually represented with symbols. Greenberg et al. (1997) asked children and adults to write the spellings of 20 words taken from a developmental spelling inventory testing multiple levels of difficulty (Bear, Truex, & Barone, 1989). They found that children spelled significantly more words correctly than adults did at all reading grade levels.

In the spelling task, words became increasingly difficult so that spellers reached a point where the words were less familiar and not represented in their lexicons. Of interest were the misspellings produced by children and adults. We expected that various factors may influence their constructions. Because children are routinely given spelling tests as part of regular school activities, they may attempt to write more words they do not know whereas adults may be more prone to leave blanks. In addition, because children were found to be more phonologically skilled than adults, they may use more graphophonemic strategies than the adults. Finally, due to the different daily writing practices of adults and children, their spelling knowledge and strategies may be different, with adults' constructions deviating from the developmental stages and strategies evident in children.

Rhyme word detection is another task that relies heavily on both phonological and orthographic knowledge. Greenberg et al. (1997) presented children and adults with Levinthal and Hornung's (1992) pairs of written words and asked them to circle all the pairs that rhymed. Results indicated that children outperformed adults across all word-reading grade levels. In this study, children's and adults' performance on each of the four types of word pairs were analyzed separately. We expected that adults may erroneously circle more pairs than children when the orthography "looked right" (i.e., words such as *have/gave*), and adults may erroneously overlook more words than children when the orthography looked wrong (i.e., words such as *fuel/mule*). We predicted that the two groups would make few errors detecting pairs such as *make/take* that rhymed and were spelled similarly. Similarly, we predicted that the two groups would make few errors on the word pairs that did not look or sound alike (e.g., *girl/jump*). These predictions were guided by the notion that because adult learners' relative strength lies in the orthographic domain, their errors in detecting rhyming words would be more influenced by orthographic cues, whereas children would be more influenced by phonological cues and thereby able to ignore the distracting orthographic cues more readily.

METHOD

Participants

Seventy-two native English-speaking adult literacy students and 72 native English-speaking children participated in the initial study (Greenberg et al., 1997); their responses were further analyzed in this study. To qualify for the study, the adults and children had to receive a word-reading score that placed them between the third- and fifth-grade reading levels on both forms of the Word Recognition subtest of the Woodcock Reading Mastery Test–Revised (Woodcock, 1987; i.e., raw scores of 105–154 words read correctly on Forms G and H). In addition, children had to score within 6 months of their expected grade-equivalent word-reading level. Children who had repeated or skipped a grade in school did not participate. None of the participants had any apparent hearing or speech difficulties. There were 24 participants at each word-reading grade level (third, fourth, fifth) in both the child and the adult groups. Analyses confirmed that the adults and children read a similar number of words at each word-reading grade level (see Table 1 for mean performances, standard deviations, and test statistics on task performance as reported by Greenberg et al.).

The adults were selected from 16 community adult basic education classes geared for grade levels 3 to 6 in the Minneapolis/St. Paul metropolitan area. Children were selected from five public elementary schools in the same neighborhoods as the adult literacy centers, with three of the five public schools housing three of the adult literacy programs that were utilized. Children selected were similar to the adults in terms of residential neighborhoods, gender, and race. More specific information regarding the characteristics of the participants can be found in Greenberg et al. (1997).

TABLE 1
Mean Performances, Standard Deviations, and Test Statistics on the Tasks
Given to Adult Literacy Students and Children

Dependent Measures	Adults		Children		Main Effect of Participant Group, $F(1, 138)$	Main Effect of Reading Level[a], $F(2, 138)$	Main Effect of Group × Level, $F(2, 138)$
	M	SD	M	SD			
Word ID	132.4	15.6	131.1	15.0	2.70	631.12*	1.93
Nonword decoding[b]	18.1	8.3	27.3	6.6	85.94*	42.35*	1.76
Sight word reading[c]	28.4	9.3	24.7	8.2	15.86*	103.09*	.97
Spelling[d]	9.3	4.2	10.9	3.8	10.15*	60.79*	.98

Note. There were 72 participants per cell. Data given as reported by Greenberg, Ehri, and Perin (1997). Mean performances, standard deviations, and test statistics on the Rhyme Word Judgment task are presented in Table 9.

[a]Reading level refers to the groups of participants reading at the third-, fourth-, and fifth-grade levels as measured by the Word Recognition subtest of the Woodcock Reading Mastery Test–Revised (Woodcock, 1987). [b]Max. $n = 40$. [c]Max. $n = 50$. [d]Max. $n = 20$.

*$p < .001$.

Materials

Responses to four tasks from the Greenberg et al. (1997) study were analyzed in this study:

1. Sight Word-Reading Task: Students were asked to read from a list of 50 atypically spelled words. This list, created by Adams and Huggins (1985), consists of words that do not follow basic spelling–sound rules and are graduated in difficulty (e.g., *sugar, aisle, ocean*). Testing was discontinued when 10 consecutive words were read incorrectly.

2. Nonword Decoding Task: To assess decoding ability, the Word Attack subtest of the Woodcock Reading Mastery Test–Revised (Woodcock, 1987) was administered. Participants were asked to read pseudowords (e.g., *oss*). The test was discontinued when participants incorrectly read six consecutive items at the end of a set.

3. Spelling Task: Bear et al.'s (1989) spelling inventory was utilized. This inventory was designed to measure growth following Henderson's (1985) stages of spelling development. It consists of 20 words that are graduated in difficulty (e.g., *bed, popping, fortunate*). Words were dictated and participants were asked to write the spelling of each word.

4. Rhyme Word Detection Task: An adaptation of Levinthal and Hornung's (1992) task was administered. Participants were presented with 212 pairs of words, and they were required to circle those pairs that rhymed. The word pairs varied in their phonological (P) and orthographic (O) similarity (S) or difference (D): OSPS words both rhymed and looked alike (*barge/large*); ODPS words rhymed but did not look alike (*fuel/mule*); OSPD words looked alike but did not rhyme (*have/gave*); ODPD words did not rhyme and did not look alike (*girl/jump*).

Error Analysis

The focus of this study was on an analysis of errors of the participants. A research assistant was trained during practice sessions with prototypes to analyze and code the responses into different categories (as explained subsequently). Her codings of actual test responses were closely monitored and checked by two of the three authors. All disagreements were resolved by discussion.

Sight word reading.   To uncover the strategies used by adults and children to read unknown real words, the errors were analyzed according to the following categories: real-word responses (e.g., stating *machine* for the stimulus word *mechanic*) and nonword responses (e.g., stating *dentee* for the stimulus word *deny*).

Nonword responses were further analyzed to see whether adults and children differed in their utilization of spelling–sound correspondence rules to produce acceptable decodings (e.g., stating *deef* for the stimulus word *deaf*). Each individual's number of errors in each category was then transformed into a proportion of the total errors the person had committed.

Nonword decoding.   Errors were coded either as a real word or a nonreal, nonsense word. The real words were then expressed as a proportion of the total nonsense plus real-word errors for each participant.

Spelling.   The spelling errors for all 20 words were assigned to five mutually exclusive categories (see Ehri, 1986): phonetic (spelling *when* as *wen*), semiphonetic (spelling *bump* as *bup*), nonphonetic (spelling *squirrel* as *chegh*), another word correctly spelled (spelling *fortunate* as *force*), and another word misspelled (spelling *inspection* as *instint*). Following Bear et al.'s (1989) exemplars listed by stage, the responses (both correct and incorrect spellings) of the final most difficult 10 words were also analyzed to see whether children's and adults' responses could be characterized by Henderson's (1985) Within Word Pattern (WWP) or Syllable Juncture (SJ) stages. Evidence of spelling words utilizing a Within Word strategy includes the utilization of short vowel patterns, such as *cot* for *caught*, whereas evidence for spelling words utilizing an SJ strategy includes the ability to spell polysyllabic words, such as *preparing* (the list of specific exemplars utilized in this analysis can be found in Bear et al.).

Rhyme word detection.   The task was to circle pairs of written words that rhymed in speech. Errors were tallied in the four categories of stimuli as previously described (OSPS, ODPS, OSPD, ODPD).

RESULTS

Results are reported separately for each task. Analyses of variance (ANOVAs) were conducted to test for differences between adults' and children's errors. Participant (adult vs. child) and word-reading grade level (third vs. fourth vs. fifth) were the independent variables. The data analyses that utilized word-reading grade-equivalency levels were based on the raw scores on the Woodcock Word Identification subtest (Woodcock, 1987). Further, when proportions were the dependent variable, the arc sine transformation was applied to transform scores.

Sight Word Reading

To place the errors within context, the data were initially analyzed to see whether adults and children differed in responding with silence or stating "I don't know" when presented with an unknown sight word. Analysis indicated that this was a common strategy used by 96% of the adults and 100% of the children (100% of both the adults and the children at the third-grade reading level; 94% of the adults and 100% of the children at the fourth-grade reading level; 94% of the adults and 100% of the children at the fifth-grade reading level).

When adults and children made errors, the adults misread more sight words as other real words than children, $F(1, 138) = 33.90, p < .001$ (see Table 2 for means and standard deviations). A main effect of word-reading grade level was detected as well, $F(2, 138) = 10.96, p < .001$. No significant interactions were noted.

In contrast, the children produced more nonwords than the adults, $F(1, 138) = 25.74, p < .001$. A main effect of word-reading grade level was detected as well, $F(2, 138) = 9.70, p < .001$, with no interactions noted (see Table 2 for means and standard deviations). Interestingly, the mean proportions of nonwords clearly increased across reading grade levels in adults, perhaps reflecting growth in phonological skills.

Further analyses were conducted on the nonword responses to see whether adults and children differed in their utilization of spelling–sound correspondence rules to produce acceptable decodings (*deef* for the stimulus word *deaf*). Results indicated that the children produced more acceptable decodings than the adults, $F(1, 138) = 36.28, p < .001$. A main effect of word-reading grade level was detected as well, $F(2, 138) = 12.02, p < .001$, with no interactions noted (see Table 2 for means and standard deviations). These results are consistent with expectations. Children were more apt to recruit phonological decoding skills to tackle words that exceeded their sight vocabularies. Because adults were less apt to decode the words as a result of weak alphabetic knowledge, they were less likely to generate nonwords. Their responses were predominantly limited to other real words that they guessed or accessed in memory based on partial letter cues.

We examined the real-word misreadings that were produced by children and adults to see whether they accessed the same or a different set of words. We found that the two groups produced the same real-word errors for 71% of these items (i.e., stating *chores* for the stimulus *chorus*; *banquet* for the stimulus *bouquet*; and *business* for the stimulus *busy*). This indicates that differences in their everyday experiences with words in the course of living as working adults or school children did not influence their choice of selection of substitute words.

Nonword Decoding

To place the errors within context, the data were initially analyzed to see whether adults and children differed in responding with silence or stating "I don't know"

TABLE 2

Sight Word Reading Responses Means and Standard Deviations

Dependent Measures	3rd-Grade Level				4th-Grade Level				5th-Grade Level				Total Adults		Total Children	
	Adults		Children		Adults		Children		Adults		Children					
	M	SD	M	SD	M	SD	M	SD	M	SD	M	SD	M	SD	M	SD
Proportion of incorrect real-word responses	.76	.16	.55	.20	.63	.17	.46	.16	.59	.15	.50	.18	.66	.17	.50	.18
Proportion of nonwords	.24	.16	.45	.19	.37	.17	.54	.16	.41	.17	.50	.17	.34	.17	.50	.17
Proportion of acceptable decodings	.18	.14	.37	.20	.32	.17	.52	.18	.37	.16	.52	.17	.29	.16	.47	.18

Note.   There were 72 participants per cell.

when presented with the nonsense words. Analysis indicated that this response was apparent in 13% of the adults and 4% of the children (17% of the adults and 6% of the children at the third-grade reading level; 14% of the adults and 6% of the children at the fourth-grade reading level; 7% of the adults and 1% of the children at the fifth-grade reading level).

In the next analysis, the proportions of errors consisting of real words were examined. As can be seen in Table 3, adults read the nonsense words as real words significantly more often than the children, $F(1, 138) = 58.60, p < .001$. This supported our expectation that as a result of impaired decoding skill, adults would rely on their knowledge of real words more than children even when given the task of reading nonwords. Fewer real-word responses occurred at higher word-reading grade levels for both groups. However this pattern was statistically significant only for the adult group, $F(2, 69) = 9.17, p < .001$. Specifically, mean errors reading nonwords as real words dropped from 42% at the third-grade level to 38% at the fourth-grade level to 25% at the fifth-grade level for adults, whereas means declined from 21% at the third-grade level to 20% at the fourth-grade level to 18% at the fifth-grade level for children.

Spelling

The percentage of adults and children who spelled each word correctly was calculated to see whether performance declined in both groups as words became harder. As can be seen in Table 4, similar to Bear et al.'s (1989) findings, the words became progressively difficult. However, the words became more difficult for adults earlier in the test than for children. The children were more accurate than the adults in spelling all but two of the words. Differences favoring children were especially large on Words 7 to 10.

Spelling errors were categorized into five types. As can be seen by Table 5, children produced significantly more phonetic misspellings than adults, $F(1, 138) = 30.44, p < .001$, at all grade levels, $F(2, 138) = 22.89, p < .001$, with no interactions noted. Phonetic misspellings increased dramatically across reading grade levels, for example, from 31% (third-grade-equivalent level) to 75% (fifth-grade-equivalent level) among adults, and from 75% (third-grade-equivalent level) to 98% (fifth-grade-equivalent level) among children.

Whereas almost all participants produced at least one phonetic misspelling, the other types of errors were produced by only some participants, so ANOVAs on the number of errors produced by individuals were not appropriate. To compare adults and children, the proportions of students producing at least one and two errors of each type were calculated and tested for significance using a z test of proportions. Results reported in Table 6 reveal that significantly more children than adults produced semiphonetic misspellings of words. However, signif-

TABLE 3
Real-Word Responses to Nonword Decoding Task

Dependent Measures	3rd-Grade Level				4th-Grade Level				5th-Grade Level				Total Adults		Total Children	
	Adults		Children		Adults		Children		Adults		Children					
	M	SD	M	SD	M	SD	M	SD	M	SD	M	SD	M	SD	M	SD
Real-word responses	.42	.16	.21	.12	.38	.16	.20	.09	.25	.10	.18	.08	.35	.16	.20	.10

Note.   There were 72 participants per cell.

TABLE 4
Percentage of Children and Adults Spelling Words Correctly

Item No. and Word	% Children[a]	% Adults[b]	% Difference[c]
1. Bed	100	100	0
2. Ship	100	94	6
3. Drive	99	92	7
4. Bump	78	75	3
5. When	92	82	10
6. Train	88	82	6
7. Closet	81	63	18
8. Chase	74	49	25
9. Float	65	49	16
10. Beaches	76	46	30
11. Preparing	33	24	9
12. Popping	44	42	2
13. Cattle	50	40	10
14. Caught	32	26	6
15. Inspection	35	26	9
16. Puncture	22	5	17
17. Cellar	19	22	-3[d]
18. Pleasure	25	32	-7[d]
19. Squirrel	13	8	5
20. Fortunate	8	4	4

[a]$n = 72$. [b]$n = 72$. [c]Percentage difference between children and adults. [d]The percentage of children spelling more words correctly was greater than the adults with the exception of Items 17 and 18.

icantly more adults than children produced misspellings that were nonphonetic. In addition, significantly more adults than children miswrote words as other words, either spelled correctly or spelled close enough to another word that we could identify the word. All of these findings parallel the decoding findings, suggesting weaker graphophonemic skills and greater use of a lexical guessing strategy among the adults.

Further analyses were undertaken to see if phonetic/semiphonetic strategies changed for adults and children as a function of difficulty of the word. Phonetic and semiphonetic errors were tabulated separately for the first 10 easier words (spelling items 1–10) and the final 10 more difficult words (spelling items 11–20). On average, 80% of the children's misspellings of the first 10 words were classified phonetic/semiphonetic and 77% of their misspelled words from the second set. By contrast, 56% of adults' misspelled words from the first 10 items were classified phonetic/semiphonetic and 52% of their misspelled words from the second set. Although proportions were lower for adults than for children, the proportions of phonetic/semiphonetic misspellings did not decline much for more difficult words.

TABLE 5
Phonetic Misspellings Means and Standard Deviations

Dependent Measure	3rd-Grade Level				4th-Grade Level				5th-Grade Level				Total Adults		Total Children	
	Adults		Children		Adults		Children		Adults		Children					
	M	SD	M	SD	M	SD	M	SD	M	SD	M	SD	M	SD	M	SD
Proportion of misspellings	.31	.24	.75	.26	.63	.39	.83	.22	.75	.36	.98	.10	.56	.38	.85	.22

Note. There were 72 participants per cell.

TABLE 6
Proportion of Adults and Children Who Produced Four Types of Spelling Errors
at Least Once and at Least Twice

	One or More Errors			Two or More Errors		
Error Type	% Adults	% Children	z	% Adults	% Children	z
Semiphonetic	51	67	1.95	14	32	2.55*
Nonphonetic	78	50	3.50**	56	24	3.95**
Another word correctly spelled	67	53	1.75	35	15	2.69**
Another word misspelled	24	11	1.98*	—	—	—

Note. There were 72 adults and 72 children. Dashes indicate too few responses.
$*z \geq 1.96, p < .05.$ $**z \geq 2.58, p < .01.$

TABLE 7
Proportion of Spellings Characterized by Within Word Patterns or Syllable Juncture

	Children			Adults		
Grade Level	WWP	SJ	Total	WWP	SJ	Total
3rd	.68	.25	.93	.52	.17	.69
4th	.46	.54	1.00	.37	.40	.77
5th	.26	.72	.98	.35	.59	.94

Note. The proportions are based on correct and incorrect spellings of the final 10 words. WWP = within word patterns; SJ = syllable juncture.

We examined spellings of the final 10 most difficult words on the list. We combined both correct and incorrect spellings and distinguished those showing knowledge of Henderson's (1985) WWP and those showing knowledge of Henderson's SJ. As can be seen in Table 7, both adults and children showed decreased use of WWP, and increased use of SJ knowledge at the higher word-reading grade levels. These findings are consistent with Henderson's stage view of spelling development.

Table 7 also presents the total mean percentages of spelling productions that could be characterized as exhibiting either WWP or SJ knowledge. From these results, we can see that values were close to 100% for the children at all word-reading grade levels but were substantially below 100% for adults at the third- and fourth-grade levels and only came close to 100% at the fifth-grade level. These results show that at the third- and fourth-grade reading levels, adults lagged behind in their spelling development gauged according to a stage view of children's spelling development.

The difference between adults' and children's production of SJ spellings was significant, $F(1, 138) = 13.40, p < .001$. Also, a main effect of word-reading grade level was detected, $F(2, 138) = 68.60, p < .001$, with no interactions noted. For WWP spellings, the picture was slightly more complex, with participant as adult or child not showing a main effect but word-reading grade showing a main effect, $F(2, 138) = 25.44, p < .001$, and an interaction between grade and participant, $F(2, 138) = 4.56, p < .01$. Post hoc analyses indicated that at the third-grade word-reading level, children produced more WWP spellings than adults, $F(1, 46) = 5.04, p < .05$, but child–adult differences were not significant at the fourth- or fifth-grade levels ($p > .05$).

As indicated by Table 7 some responses by the adults and children could not be characterized by either the WW or SJ spelling stages. Further analyses were conducted to see how many responses could be characterized as examples of Henderson's (1985) prephonetic stage (i.e., writing only the first, last, or first and last sounds of a word). The percentage of individuals spelling at least one of the last 10 words prephonetically was computed. As can be seen in Table 8 the children and adults showed different patterns. The children showed very little use of a prephonetic strategy. In contrast, 25% to 46% of the adults used this strategy on at least one of the final 10 words. However, because no strategy reports were collected, it is also possible that the adults were not using a prephonetic strategy but had simply given up trying to spell words they did not know. This may be supported by the analysis that was undertaken to explore whether adults and children left responses blank. All participants were told that if they do not know how to spell a word, they should try their best and guess if necessary. Thirty-three percent of the adults at the third-grade word-reading level, 25% of the adults at the fourth-grade level, and 8% of the adults at the fifth-grade level left at least one word unspelled. Not one child left a word unspelled. This suggests that adults were less apt than children to attempt to construct spellings that they did not know.

Rhyme Word Detection

As indicated by total correct scores in Table 9, children were more successful at detecting rhyming words than the adults were. This was true at all grade levels.

TABLE 8
Percentage of Children and Adults Spelling at Least One Word Prephonetically

Word-Reading Grade Level	% Children[a]	% Adults[b]
3rd	13	42
4th	0	46
5th	4	25

[a]$n = 72$. [b]$n = 72$.

TABLE 9
Rhyming Word Means, Standard Deviations, and Test Statistics in the Analyses of Variance

Dependent Measures	Adults		Children		Main Effect of Participant Group, $F(1, 138)$	Main Effect of Reading Level, $F(2, 138)$	Group × Level, $F(2, 138)$
	M	SD	M	SD			
Total correct[a]	140.88	22.89	158.22	20.77	28.61**	19.23**	1.53
OSPS errors[b] (make/take)	14.22	12.11	6.62	7.08	22.46**	5.81*	.805
OSPD errors[b] (have/gave)	22.09	12.34	22.33	10.19	.016	3.64*	1.74
ODPS errors[b] (fuel/mule)	27.27	12.66	18.76	11.17	20.92**	10.67**	1.50
ODPD errors[b] (girl/jump)	8.03	9.18	6.54	5.65	1.36	1.50	.14

Note. There were 72 participants per cell. OSPS = orthographically similar, phonologically similar; OSPD = orthographically similar, phonologically different; ODPS = orthographically different, phonologically similar; ODPD = orthographically different, phonologically different.
[a]Max. $n = 212$. [b]Max. $n = 53$.
*$p < .05$. **$p < .001$.

No differences were found between children and adults on the ODPD (*girl/jump*) word pairs. This indicates that both groups were equally skilled at detecting words that clearly did not rhyme in spelling or in speech. For both adults and children, OSPS (*make/take*), OSPD (*have/gave*), and ODPS (*fuel/mule*) errors decreased at higher grade levels. However, at all grade levels, the most frequent type of error differed for adults and children, with adults overlooking rhymes spelled differently most often (*fuel/mule*) and children falling for similar spellings representing nonrhyming words most often (*have/gave*). Thus, the adults had the most difficulty determining that pairs of orthographically different words rhymed, whereas children had the greatest difficulty determining that orthographically similar words did not rhyme. In addition, as evident in Table 9, adults made many more errors on OSPS pairs (*make/take*) than children. One explanation is that adults were not as skilled as children were in accessing phonological representations of words to judge whether they rhymed when the spelling signaled a possible rhyme. Another explanation is that children were more biased than adults to circle words with the same spelling pattern.

Both children's performance and adults' performance were above chance levels (i.e., 50%) on rhyming words cued by similar spellings (adults = an average of 73% correct; children = an average of 88% correct) and on nonrhyming words with similar spellings (both adults and children = an average of 58% correct). However, the adults' performance on orthographically dissimilar rhymes (*fuel/mule*) did not differ from chance (i.e., 49% correct), whereas children's performance was above chance level (i.e., 65% correct).

DISCUSSION

This study shows that adult literacy students and children tended to differ not only quantitatively in reading and spelling words (Greenberg et al., 1997) but also qualitatively. In other words, the groups differed not only in error rate as found in the initial Greenberg et al. study but also in error types. This finding suggests that adult literacy students and children tend to utilize different cognitive processes and approaches to the tasks, possibly with the use of compensatory strategies. Findings were consistent in showing that when encountering difficulties in sight word reading, nonword reading, spelling, and rhyme word detection, adults were not as likely as children to use spelling–sound correspondences and phonological decoding processes to help them, but rather were more likely to rely on visual memory to produce responses. This is not surprising because the adults' decoding skills were much weaker than those of the children (Greenberg et al., 1997).

Results of the spelling analyses indicated that although a similar pattern of progressive difficulty was apparent for both children and adults, the words became more difficult for adults earlier in the test. This is consistent with other findings indicating that disabled readers are especially poor spellers (Bruck, 1993; Ehri, 1997). In addition, results revealed that adults exhibited some spellings resembling those described by Henderson (1985) as prephonetic and found at an early stage of spelling development. Whereas children spelled few if any words prephonetically, 25% to 46% of the adults showed this pattern on at least one of the words. It is possible that the adults wrote one letter and then gave up writing the rest of the word. This explanation is consistent with the fact that many adults left words blank on the test, whereas not one child left a word unspelled. Adults may not be used to spelling unfamiliar words, whereas children are commonly encouraged to spell words they do not know and therefore have more practice using a sounding out strategy to help them. Leaving words blank, or only writing one or two letters may be a way that adult literacy students avoid difficulty and embarrassment at their lack of spelling knowledge. In future studies, a spelling recognition task may be less intimidating to adults, as compared to the spelling production task utilized in this study.

In the Greenberg et al. (1997) study, children were reported to outperform adults on the rhyme word detection task. Scores used in that study were limited to the word pairs with discrepant spellings and sounds (i.e., OSPD and ODPS pairs). The present error analysis revealed that the difference favoring children arose solely from the ODPS word pairs (*mule/fuel*), not the OSPD pairs (*have/gave*), which did not distinguish the two groups (see Table 9). That is, adults had more problems than children only when the spellings of rhyming words were dissimilar, not when the spellings of nonrhyming words were similar. However, a response bias to circle similarly spelled words may have boosted children's errors on the OSPD words.

Our explanation for the pattern of errors observed in the rhyme detection task is based on the propensities of adult disabled readers to rely more on orthographic processing and normally developing child readers to rely more on phonological decoding processes. Adults performed at chance level in judging rhyming pairs with different spellings (*mule/fuel*) but performed at above-chance levels in judging pairs with similar spellings (*take/make* and *have/gave*). Very likely this occurred because adults paid primary attention to the orthography as a cue indicating a potential rhyming sound. In contrast, children applied a decoding strategy to process the pairs of words. This made them very accurate on words with similar spellings and rhyming sounds (*take/make*) but less accurate when spellings were similar but the sounds did not rhyme (*have/gave*) and when sounds were similar but spellings were different (*mule/fuel*).

The adults in this study appear to resemble Ehri's (1987, 1989, 1991) phonetic cue readers and to process words differently from younger normally developing readers at the same word-reading level. Phonetic cue readers use partial alphabetic cues to help them read words rather than a phonological recoding strategy. Rather than work out the pronunciations of words from their spellings, they tend to guess the identities of words based on shared letters in spellings. Evidence from this study indicates that the adults were less likely to employ graphophonemic correspondences to complete the tasks in contrast to children. Adults' chance-level performance in judging rhyming words with different spellings (*fuel/mule*) is consistent with Ehri's (1997) assertion that spellings of words are not fully amalgamated with pronunciations in the lexical memories of disabled readers but rather are only partially connected to pronunciations. The partial connections typically involve consonants but not vowels. This may create more ambiguity in the identity of vowels in words for poor readers than for normal readers who know the regularities of vowel spellings and use these to fully connect spellings in memory. Because poor readers know less about alternative ways that vowels are spelled, they fail to recognize equivalences among variable spelling patterns.

The adults' reliance on orthography over phonology is similar to patterns found in other special populations. For example, Temple and Marshall (1983) conducted a case study of a 17-year-old developmental dyslexic who was observed to produce real-word errors in response to nonword stimuli. Juel and Roper/Schneider (1985) observed that beginning readers with weak decoding skills remembered how to read unusual words with distinctive letters more easily than words resembling other words in letter structure. In addition, Siegel, Share, and Geva (1995) found that learning disabled children exhibited stronger letter pattern knowledge but weaker phonological skills. They proposed that in learning to read, disabled readers compensate for their weak phonological skills by relying more heavily on orthographic processes than nondisabled readers in learning to read. That is, they concentrate on remembering letter sequences apart from their phonological function more so than nondisabled readers do. The results of this study support a similar explanation of low-literate adults' word-reading behaviors.

Although differences between children and adults were highlighted in this study, two similarities are interesting. Results from the rhyme word detection task indicated that both adults and children were heavily influenced by the rule that if two words look alike, they probably rhyme. These findings suggest an awareness in both groups of the tendency of rhyming words to have the same letter patterns in the English spelling system.

In addition, it was interesting that on those sight words that were misread as other real words, both adults and children produced the same real-word errors for 71% of the items. It was hypothesized that due to different experiences with words, the groups would produce different words. The fact that adults did not differ from children in the particular words that were substituted when they misread sight words as other real words indicates that exposure to different types of words on a daily basis was not influential. Rather orthographic cues were more likely the determining factor.

Although applying the word-reading grade level concept to adults is controversial (e.g., Perin, 1991), it was employed as an independent variable in this study because no better metric on which both children and adults may be measured is available. The interaction effect that was found for the spelling task bears on this issue. For example, adult–child differences in the utilization of WWP spelling strategies were only found at the third-grade word-reading level and not at the fourth- and fifth-grade levels. Similarly, Greenberg et al. (1997) found an interaction effect on a receptive vocabulary test. They found that adults outperformed children at the third- and fourth-grade levels but not at the fifth-grade level. These findings suggest that adults and children may be more different at the beginning levels in acquiring word-reading and spelling capabilities, but as they continue to develop some of the differences may begin to fade away. Clearly more research is needed to compare adults and children at higher word-reading levels to see if this trend continues. In addition, longitudinal research is warranted to explore the replicability of these cross-sectional findings.

Two directions are recommended for future studies. It is important to understand the impact of instructional history on task performance. It is possible that a confound in this study is that the instructional histories of the two groups differed and therefore the error patterns of both groups reflect their learning environments more than their innate skills or strategy preferences. It would have been informative to investigate whether the types of strategies the elementary school and adult literacy teachers taught and encouraged when difficulties were encountered in reading and spelling differed for the children and adults. Similarly, future researchers may want to include think-aloud procedures while participants are engaged in the tasks. Although many clues are derived from behavioral observations, much more can be gained by eavesdropping on the thought processes that occur before the behavioral response. This may have proved informative in the rhyme detection task. We may have found that adults first checked to see if the words were spelled similarly at their ends and if so, they then tried to find acceptable pronunciations that made the words rhyme. A think-aloud procedure may permit this type of hypothesis testing.

ACKNOWLEDGMENTS

We thank Alpana Bhattacharya for her assistance in coding the data.

REFERENCES

Adams, M. J., & Huggins, A. W. F. (1985). The growth of children's sight vocabulary: A quick test with educational and theoretical implications. *Reading Research Quarterly, 20,* 262–281.

Bear, D. R., Truex, P., & Barone, D. (1989). In search of meaningful diagnosis: Spelling-by-stage assessment of literacy proficiency. *Adult Literacy and Basic Education, 3,* 165–185.

Bruck, M. (1993). Component spelling skills of college students with childhood diagnoses of dyslexia. *Learning Disability Quarterly, 16,* 171–184.

Castro-Caldas, A., Petersson, K. M., Reis, A., Stone-Elander, S., & Ingvar, M. (1998). The illiterate brain: Learning to read and write during childhood influences the functional organization of the adult brain. *Brain, 121,* 1053–1063.

Ehri, L. C. (1986). Sources of difficulty in learning to spell and read. In M. L. K. Wolraich & D. Routh (Eds.), *Advances in developmental and behavioral pediatrics* (pp. 121–195). Greenwich, CT: JAI.

Ehri, L. C. (1987). Learning to read and spell words. *Journal of Reading Behavior, 19,* 5–31.

Ehri, L. C. (1989). The development of spelling knowledge and its role in reading acquisition and reading disability. *Journal of Learning Disabilities, 22,* 356–365.

Ehri, L. C. (1991). Development of the ability to read words. In R. Barr, M. Kamil, P. Mosenthal, & P. D. Pearson (Eds.), *Handbook of reading research* (Vol. 2, pp. 383–417). Mahwah, NJ: Lawrence Erlbaum Associates, Inc.

Ehri, L. (1997). Learning to read and learning to spell are one and the same, almost. In C. Perfetti, L. Rieben, & M. Fayol (Eds.), *Learning to spell: Research, theory and practice across languages* (pp. 237–269). Mahwah, NJ: Lawrence Erlbaum Associates, Inc.

Fawcett, A., & Nicholson, R. (1995). Persistence of phonological awareness deficits in older children with dyslexia. *Reading and Writing: An Interdisciplinary Journal, 7,* 361–376.

Frith, U. (1985). Beneath the surface of developmental dyslexia. In K. Patterson, M. Coltheart, & J. Marshall (Eds.), *Surface dyslexia: Neuropsychological and cognitive studies of phonological reading* (pp. 301–330). Hillsdale, NJ: Lawrence Erlbaum Associates, Inc.

Goldsmith-Phillips, J. (1994). Toward a research-based dyslexia assessment. In N. C. Jordan & J. Goldsmith-Phillips (Eds.), *Learning disabilities: New directions for assessment and intervention* (pp. 85–100). Boston: Allyn & Bacon.

Gottesman, R. L., Bennett, R. E., Nathan, R. G., & Kelly, M. S. (1996). Inner-city adults with severe reading difficulties: A closer look. *Journal of Learning Disabilities, 29,* 589–597.

Gough, P. B., & Tunmer, W. E. (1986). Decoding, reading, and reading disability. *Remedial and Special Education, 7,* 6–10.

Greenberg, D., Ehri, L., & Perin, D. (1997). Are word-reading processes the same or different in adult literacy students and third–fifth graders matched for reading level? *Journal of Educational Psychology, 89,* 262–275.

Henderson, E. H. (1985). *Teaching spelling.* Boston: Houghton Mifflin.

Iribarren, I. C., Jarema, G., & Lecours, A. R. (1999). Lexical reading in Spanish: Two cases of phonological dyslexia. *Applied Psycholinguistics, 20,* 407–428.

Juel, C., & Roper/Schneider, D. (1985). The influence of basal readers on first grade reading. *Reading Research Quarterly, 20,* 134–152.

Kirsch, I., Jungeblut, A., Jenkins, L., & Kolstad, A. (1993). *Findings from the 1992 National Adult Literacy Survey.* Washington, DC: U.S. Department of Education, National Center for Education Statistics. (ERIC Document Reproduction Service No. ED358375)

Levinthal, C., & Hornung, M. (1992). Orthographic and phonological coding during visual word matching as related to reading and spelling abilities in college students. *Reading and Writing: An Interdisciplinary Journal, 4,* 231–244.

Liberman, I. Y., Rubin, H., Duques, S., & Carlisle, J. (1985). Linguistic abilities and spelling proficiency in kindergartners and adult poor spellers. In D. B. Gray & J. F. Kavanagh (Eds.), *Biobehavioral measures of dyslexia* (pp. 163–176). Parkton, MD: York Press.

Lindamood, P. C., Bell, N., & Lindamood, P. (1992). Issues in phonological awareness assessment. *Annals of Dyslexia, 42,* 242–259.

Marsh, G., Friedman, M., Welch, V., & Desberg, P. (1981). A cognitive development theory of reading acquisition. In G. E. McKinnon & T. G. Waller (Eds.), *Reading research: Advances in theory and practice* (Vol. 3, pp. 199–221). New York: Academic.

Moats, L. C. (1993). Spelling error interpretation: Beyond the phonetic/dysphonetic dichotomy. *Annals of Dyslexia, 43,* 174–183.

Perfetti, C., & Marron, M. (1995). *Learning to read: Literacy acquisition by children and adults* (Report No. NCAL–TR–95–07). Philadelphia: National Center on Adult Literacy. (ERIC Document Reproduction Service No. ED396155)

Perin, D. (1991). Test scores and adult literacy instruction: Relationship of reading test scores to three types of literacy instruction in a worker education program. *Language and Literacy Spectrum, 1,* 46–51.

Perin, D. (1998). Assessing the reading-writing relation in adult literacy students. *Reading Psychology, 19,* 141–184.

Sawyer, D. J., Wade, S., & Kim, J. K. (1999). Spelling errors as a window on variations in phonological deficits among students with dyslexia. *Annals of Dyslexia, 49,* 137–159.

Shaughnessy, M. P. (1977). *Errors and expectations: A guide for the teacher of basic writing.* New York: Oxford University Press.

Siegel, L., Share, D., & Geva, E. (1995). Evidence for superior orthographic skills in dyslexics. *Psychological Science, 6,* 250–254.

Snow, C. E., & Strucker, J. (2000). Lessons from preventing reading difficulties in young children for adult learning and literacy. In J. Comings, B. Garner, & C. Smith (Eds.), *The annual review of adult learning and literacy* (Vol. 1, pp. 25–73). San Francisco: Jossey Bass.

Snowling, M. J. (2000). *Dyslexia.* Malden, MA: Blackwell.

Temple, C. M., & Marshall, J. C. (1983). A case study of developmental phonological dyslexia. *British Journal of Psychology, 74,* 517–533.

Woodcock, R. N. (1987). *Woodcock Reading Mastery Test–Revised.* Circle Pines, MN: American Guidance Service.

Worthy, J., & Viise, N. M. (1996). Morphological, phonological and orthographic differences between the spelling of normally achieving children and basic literacy students. *Reading and Writing: An Interdisciplinary Journal, 8,* 139–159.

Manuscript received May 4, 2001
Final revision received December 1, 2001
Accepted December 4, 2001

SCIENTIFIC STUDIES OF READING, 6(3), 245–266
Copyright © 2002, Lawrence Erlbaum Associates, Inc.

Phonological Awareness in Literacy Acquisition: It's Not Only for Children

Aydin Yücesan Durgunoğlu

University of Minnesota Duluth

Banu Öney

University of Illinois at Chicago

The aim of this study was to determine the cognitive processes of adult literacy acqui-sition. We assessed the progress of 59 women participating in an intensive adult liter-acy program that we have developed in Turkey. After only 90 hr of instruction, there were significant improvements in letter and word recognition, phonological aware-ness, and spelling levels. Word recognition and spelling were predicted by phonologi-cal awareness. The results were consistent with studies on children's literacy acquisi-tion, which show the critical nature of phonological awareness in literacy acquisition.

Considering that literacy is one of the most basic life skills, it is disconcerting to ob-serve dramatic differences in literacy levels around the world, such as between de-veloped and developing countries and between men and women (Ramdas, 1989). As Greaney (1996) documented, developed countries report illiteracy rates of 3.3%, whereas this rate is more than 30% in developing countries. However, even in developed countries the low illiteracy rates are deceiving, because there are large segments in populations who, although not illiterate, still have literacy skills too low to meet the demands of their society (see Kirsch, 1993).

There have been many national campaigns and large-scale efforts to increase the literacy levels, for example, in India, Tanzania, Brazil, Nicaragua, and Cuba (for a review, see Arnove & Graff, 1987). These campaigns usually report global outcome measures, such as the number of people reached by the campaign, and re-late literacy acquisition to such variables as fertility, health care, and economic de-

Requests for reprints should be sent to A. Y. Durgunoğlu, Department of Psychology, University of Minnesota Duluth, 1207 Ordean Court, Duluth, MN 55812.

velopment (Ballara, 1992; Gillette, 1987). However, there are very few studies investigating literacy acquisition at the level of the individuals. Most research is conducted to evaluate policies rather than the development of the participants. As Abadzi (1995) stated, "Though countless policy and methodological documents have been published, almost no rigorous research has been undertaken [on adult literacy acquisition]" (p. 3).

Currently, we have a rich knowledge base on cognitive processes in child literacy acquisition (for a review, see Adams, 1990). Many contemporary models of literacy acquisition recognize two semiautonomous cognitive components of skilled reading: (a) linguistic competence as operationalized by listening comprehension and (b) decoding, reflecting an understanding of how spoken language is represented in written form, as indicated by both word-recognition and spelling performance. Thus, to become literate, children need to understand both the spoken language and how it is represented in its written form (Gough & Tunmer, 1986; Hoover & Tunmer, 1993; Juel, Griffith, & Gough, 1986). These processes constitute the "building blocks" of reading development (Öney & Durgunoğlu, 1997). Of course these processes operate within the contexts of an individual's home and schooling experiences, basic cognitive and metacognitive proficiencies, as well as the language background (Durgunoğlu, 2001). Difficulties in the operation of building blocks, especially in decoding, lead to slow or inaccurate word recognition which in turn results in comprehension failure (Shankweiler, 1989).

Decoding depends on the discovery of the alphabetic principle, the realization that phonemes, the smallest units constituting spoken language, correspond to letters in the printed word. Phonological awareness is the key process in this discovery and refers to the ability to recognize and manipulate sublexical speech segments at the level of syllables, onset-rimes, and phonemes (Treiman, 1991). Researchers have convincingly demonstrated the link between phonological awareness and decoding skills in English (for reviews, see Adams, 1990; Goswami & Bryant, 1990). Phonological awareness is also a significant predictor of decoding in other languages (Durgunoğlu, Nagy, & Hancin-Bhatt, 1993; Wimmer, Landerl, Linortner, & Hummer, 1991) even when a language has very systematic mappings between phonemes and graphemes as is the case in Turkish (Durgunoğlu & Öney, 1999).

Phonological awareness has been repeatedly found to be a predictor of future reading ability (Liberman, 1989; Maclean, Bryant, & Bradley, 1988; Vellutino & Scanlon, 1988). Furthermore, training studies have shown that explicit instruction in phonological awareness leads to gains not only in this metalinguistic skill but also in general reading ability (Ball & Blachman, 1991). Arguments on the causal nature of the link between phonological awareness and reading acquisition continue, but the reciprocal nature of the relation is well established. As for the other building block, listening comprehension, although it does not have the same strong link to word-recognition and spelling proficiencies, it influences reading comprehension. As decoding becomes fluent, proficiencies tapped by listening comprehension may have a bigger impact on reading comprehension. For example, Oakhill (1994) discussed readers who are fluent decoders but still have problems with integrating and comprehending texts.

The question posed in this study is whether adult literacy acquisition is affected by the same factors that govern the acquisition of literacy skills in young children. Some researchers assume that cognitive processes in literacy acquisition are similar in children and adults (Chall, 1987; Perfetti & Marron, 1995) and that differences between children and adults are due to motivational, social, and contextual factors. However, it is also possible that fundamental differences in literacy acquisition for adults and children can exist because of differences in language skills and world knowledge (Perin, 1988) or cognitive processing speed (Salthouse, 1994). As an example, adults have more experience and background knowledge about the world and have proficiencies that enable them to function in a society even though their literacy skills may be limited. However, experience and background knowledge may not be very useful in the initial stages of literacy acquisition. Studies have shown that adults who cannot identify words quickly and accurately have poor comprehension levels (Curtis, 1980). Hence variables such as world knowledge and experience, which help comprehension, may not have a chance to operate, reducing any advantages adults may have over children.

One common source of difficulty for adults as well as children with limited literacy levels is awareness of phonemes. Several studies with illiterate adults in Portugal (Morais, Cary, Alegria, & Bertelson, 1979; Morais, Content, Bertelson, & Cary, 1988) demonstrated their poor performance on tasks requiring phonological manipulations. Similar results have been obtained with illiterate speakers of Serbo-Croatian (Lukatela, Carello, Shankweiler, & Liberman, 1995). Greenberg, Ehri, and Perin (1997) observed that, compared to children matched for reading age, adults with limited literacy skills had poorer phonological processing assessed by tasks such as phoneme deletion and segmentation. Pratt and Brady (1988) also reported poor phoneme deletion performance in adult literacy students. How does such limited phonological awareness affect literacy acquisition in adults? Are those processes crucial for effective literacy acquisition in adults as is the case in children, or can the adults with more developed linguistic and world knowledge follow a different path of literacy acquisition?

There are three reasons why we can expect child and adult literacy acquisition to follow similar cognitive paths. First, richer experience and background knowledge of the adults may not contribute to the basic decoding processing other than indirectly. Studies have shown that listening comprehension—as a proxy for language comprehension and background knowledge—is directly related to reading comprehension but not to word recognition. Second, as previously discussed, if basic decoding proficiency is limited, reading comprehension suffers, thus circumventing any help from the existing knowledge base. Therefore, linguistic proficiencies of adults may not be useful for basic word recognition, spelling processes, or comprehension. A third issue is more basic: The assumption that adult linguistic proficiencies are better than those of children can be questioned. Adult linguistic proficiency may plateau and not develop further in the absence of support from written materials. Researchers (Cunningham & Stanovich, 1991; Stanovich & Cunningham, 1993) have shown that the amount of exposure to written materials is a strong predictor of vocabulary development and general knowledge. Adults who cannot use written materials are likely to have less developed linguistic proficiencies. In fact, Greenberg et al. (1997) found that when matched with children of the same reading levels, adults showed higher levels of vocabulary compared to third- and fourth-grade children but lost this edge when compared to fifth-grade children. (This pattern, of course, may also be due to the familiarity with decontextualized language and test savvy acquired in school rather than the actual vocabulary size.) To summarize, although literacy acquisition may involve similar cognitive processes in both adults and children, at this point, based on inadequate data, we can only assume them to be similar. Such a gap in our knowledge base not only can cause problems in our theoretical understanding of adult literacy acquisition but also can hinder effective program development and implementation.

Studies of adult literacy acquisition, especially in the United States, have typically focused on low-literate adults who have attended school but for various reasons did not complete their education. Such research introduces an added layer of complexity, that is, whether these adults have specific learning or reading disabilities or are second language learners (Sabatini, 1999). Very few studies (Lukatela et al., 1995; Morais et al., 1979) have been conducted with truly nonliterate individuals who have had minimal exposure to print because of social and economic constraints rather than cognitive or linguistic difficulties. A more informative comparison of adult and child literacy acquisition can be obtained by investigating individuals whose first language is the majority language and who have no known cognitive impairments. Our goal in this study was to begin to address this gap in the literature and report a study on the cognitive processes of literacy acquisition by adults who never attended school but who have participated in an intensive literacy program.

In this article we investigate the literacy acquisition of a group of adult literacy participants in the Functional Adult Literacy Program (FALP), a basic adult literacy program that we have developed in Turkey. The program, currently starting its 13th cohort, has reached more than 20,000 participants, mostly women. Characteristics of FALP and its evaluation have been discussed elsewhere (Durgunoğlu, 2000; Durgunoğlu, Öney, & Kuscul, 1995, 2002). To summarize briefly, FALP is a 90-hr program[1] taught by volunteer teachers who undergo an intensive training seminar. Volunteers are supported by observers who provide feedback and create a network among the groups of teachers.

Each unit of FALP starts with a text depicting an event in the life of a family, with a picture above it. Before reading the text, the participants discuss the picture and relate it to personal experiences. Then, the text is read, accompanied by discussions and comprehension exercises. However, FALP also includes explicit instruction on letter–sound correspondences and syllabification, especially exploiting the systematicities in the Turkish orthography as well as the characteristics of its morphological structure.

Turkish has a transparent orthography with very consistent phoneme–grapheme mappings. This facilitates the acquisition of word recognition (Öney & Goldman, 1984). However, it is an agglutinating language, morphologically very complex, with many inflections added to a word to mark aspects such as tense, plurality, and so on (Aksu-Koc & Slobin, 1986; Durgunoğlu, in press). The morphological complexity makes word recognition more difficult, but help comes from the systematic syllabification rules. Syllables divide long words into manageable chunks and even override the morphological boundaries. For example, the root word *top* (ball) takes the inflection *a* to make it dative *topa* (to the ball). However, the word is syllabified as *to-pa*, thus overriding the morphemic boundaries of *top-a*, and making the syllable a very salient unit. Syllables are also very salient because of their consistency. There are only seven syllable types of consonant (C) and vowel (V) combinations (V, CV, VC, CVC, CVCC, VCC, CCVC) with CV and CVC being the most common types.

Ironically, the literacy instruction in the Turkish elementary schools does not take into consideration the characteristics of the language and its transparent orthography. In first grade, children are given sentences to memorize, and, only after memorizing the whole, the components such as individual words, syllables, and letters are identified. Despite this holistic, "going from the whole method," children, on the average, figure out the spelling–sound correspondences in this transparent orthography by the 5th month of the first grade, as evidenced by children getting their "red ribbons," signifying good decoding skills by December and January of the school year.

In FALP because we do not have the luxury of time, we provide explicit instruction on spelling–sound correspondences. We use the systematicities in language to facilitate word recognition and spelling. We explicitly teach the spelling–sound correspondences and then practice blending these individual sounds/letters into

---

[1]The 90-hr length was imposed by the Ministry of Education. Our evaluation data (Durgunoğlu et al., 2002) indicated that this is unrealistic, and, starting with Cohort 3, we have extended the program to 120 hr. However, the data in this article are based on participants from Cohort 1 who completed the original 90-hr program.

syllables. In every class period, first there are oral exercises with four individual sounds (two vowels and two consonants; e.g., *a, e, n, t*) and how they are combined into syllables (e.g., *an, at, na, ta, ne*). Then these sounds are represented by letters and the syllables are written. These syllables are then used to read and write words (e.g., *nane, tane*). As the class progresses, there is also explicit instruction in syllabification to facilitate the breaking down of long and complex words. During the 1st month of classes, almost 70% of the class time is spent on this type of instruction. During the 2nd and 3rd months of classes, the reading comprehension activities gain prominence, and about 40% of the class time is used to read and discuss passages, poems, and plays.

In addition to word recognition, spelling, and reading comprehension activities, FALP also includes functional activities such as reading and discussing newspaper articles, recognizing parts of bills, and reading product labels. Through the whole course, cooperation, active learning, and critical thinking are encouraged and built into the activities.

The first cohort of FALP included 175 participants. In this study, we focused on a subset of this cohort for in-depth assessment and documentation of the participants' literacy acquisition. We used a longitudinal design, documenting their cognitive processes at the beginning and end of the course, to assess whether the typical predictors of literacy acquisition in children, such as letter recognition and phonological awareness, operate in adult participants as well. To go back to the original model, we predicted that both listening comprehension and decoding proficiency would contribute to reading comprehension performance of adults. Decoding, as assessed by both word recognition and spelling, was assumed to be affected by phonological awareness, replicating the pattern found in research on children. In addition, letter knowledge was predicted to be a significant facilitator of decoding as well as phonological awareness.

METHOD

Participants

The participants were 59 women randomly selected from the five classes in the first cohort. They were native speakers of Turkish and had no reported cognitive impairments. Their mean age was 38.5 ($SD = 7.8$), ranging from 29 to 66. Although the majority was born in small villages, they reported living in Istanbul for an average of 20.96 ($SD = 10.0$) years. Of the participants, 98% were homemakers, 91.5% were married, and they had an average of 3.31 children. Their self-reports indicated that they had not had any formal schooling.

Tasks

The participants were assessed in the beginning and at the end of the courses, henceforth labeled as pretests and posttests, respectively. The participants were assessed individually in their homes or in the classrooms by female testers. In this article, we discuss only the subset of tasks related to cognitive processes of literacy acquisition. Because standardized tests were not available, we have created the tests. Several pretests and posttests were identical. However, in some instances, we also included posttests that were more detailed and difficult than the pretests to have a more stringent test of growth.

Pretests

Letter recognition.   The Turkish alphabet has 29 letters. The participants were asked to identify the 29 uppercase and 29 lowercase letters on a single page. The measure was the number of letters identified correctly either by name or sound.

Word recognition.   The participants were given 12 short words, reflecting the variety of vowel and consonant combinations found in Turkish. Because of the transparent orthography, the frequency of orthographic patterns was not an issue. In fact, in our previous studies, we have seen that word- and nonword-recognition performances are highly correlated (Öney & Durgunoğlu, 1997). However, words vary in difficulty as a function of the number of syllables and, of course, the number of letters. Hence, in this task both the number of letters and syllables were manipulated. There were three monosyllabic (CVC) words and nine bisyllabic words, representing the common syllable combinations of CV-CV, V-CVC, CV-CVC, and CVC-CVC. Also, care was taken to ensure that the words represented familiar concepts and objects, for example, *kuş* 'bird', *dere* 'stream', *kitap* 'book'. If any of the participants did not recognize more than 10 letters in the previous test, they were not given this task.

Spelling.   The participants were asked to spell 12 words, 3 to 10 letters long (see the Appendix). The number of correct spellings was recorded. Half of the words were in their simple form and half had inflections, hence the words in the spelling task were more difficult than the words in the recognition task. Overall, both the uninflected and inflected words had different combinations of the most common syllabic structures CVC and CV, such as CV-CVC (e.g., *savaş* 'war'), CVC-CVC (e.g., *terlik* 'slipper'), or CVC-CVC-CVC (e.g., *kamyonlar* 'trucks'). It must be noted that these long words are not unusual because of the highly inflected nature of Turkish. However, if any of the participants did not recognize more than 10 letters or read more than 5 words, they were not given this task.

Phonological awareness.   This test included three subtasks: phoneme tapping, phoneme blending, and deleting the initial and final phoneme. In the phoneme-tapping task, there were 12 words with a range of three to six phonemes, and the participants tapped the number of phonemes that they heard. In the phoneme-blending task, the participants were given 11 segmented words with a range of three to six phonemes and asked to say the word together as a whole. The initial and final phoneme deletion tasks had 12 words each, with a range of three to five phonemes. Participants were asked to say the words with their initial or final phoneme deleted.

Listening comprehension.   The participants listened to two short passages—instructions for a prescription medicine and an advertisement for a rental property—read by the experimenter and answered six questions about each passage. The questions did not require any inferencing, but did require direct recall of facts, such as how often the medicine should be taken according to the instructions and how much the rent was according to the advertisement. The participants were reminded to answer the questions based on the passage they heard.

Because the participants had very low levels of letter and word recognition, no reading comprehension test was given.

Posttests

Letter recognition.   This test was identical to the one given as a pretest (Task 1).

Word recognition (old words).   The 12 words given in the pretest were shown again (Task 2).

Word recognition (fast).   Fifteen 3-letter words (CVC) were given, and the participants were asked to read these as quickly as possible. Although this task was timed, only the accuracy data were analyzed.

Word recognition (new words).   The participants were given 12 words ranging from 4 to 12 letters in length, including some highly inflected items. There was one monosyllabic item that had an unusual structure (CVCC), reflecting the only case in Turkish in which consonant clusters are allowed. There were three bisyllabic items (V-CVC, CV-CVC, CVC-CVC), three 3-syllable items (CV-CVC-CVC, CV-CVC-CV, CV-CVC-CVC), and five 4-syllable items created by various combinations of the syllables CVC and CV.

Spelling.   The words given in the pretest spelling task were used again. However, because writing sometimes took painfully long, only 9 of the original 12 words were included in this task.

Phonological awareness.   The same tasks as in the pretest phonological awareness task were used.

Reading comprehension.   The participants were given a 75-word passage on air pollution in Istanbul. That passage was also provided in a form with words separated into syllables. The participants could read either version as they preferred. After reading the text aloud, without looking back at the text, they orally answered six questions such as "When is the pollution the heaviest?" and "Who are affected the most by pollution?" The questions required very little inferencing because the required information for all questions was readily found in the text. This task had a reliability (Cronbach's alpha) of .82

RESULTS

In the descriptive results section, we first present the means, standard deviations, and percentage accuracy on the tasks to highlight the growth in literacy skills of the participants. Then, in the correlations and multiple regression sections, we discuss how this growth is related to the predictor variables of interest.

Descriptive Statistics

Pretests

It is clear from the mean performance levels in Table 1 that the participants had very low levels of literacy skills when they started the course, recognizing only 39 of the 58 letters and 5 of the 12 common words. (The maximum possible score for

TABLE 1
Means and Standard Deviations of the Assessment Tasks

	Pretests					Posttests			
Task	Maximum	M	SD	%	Task	Maximum	M	SD	%
Letter recognition	58	39.1	18.3	67.0	Letter recognition	58	51.3	7.5	88.4
Word recognition	12	4.85	4.8	40.4	Word recognition (old)	12	9.03	3.5	75.2
					Word recognition (fast)	15	9.3	4.7	62.0
					Word recognition (new)	12	8.14	3.3	67.8
					Word recognition total	39	26.68	9.5	68.4
Spelling	12	1.10	2.1	12.2[a]	Spelling	9	2.98	2.4	33.0
Phonological awareness	47	16.56	8.1	35.0	Phonological awareness	47	22.14	9.7	47.0
Listening comprehension	12	3.02	2.0	25.1					
					Reading comprehension	6	2.82	2.1	47.0

[a]The percentage correct for the first spelling test was computed over 9 items to facilitate comparison with the second spelling test because the second test included only 9 of the original 12 items.

each task is given in the parentheses.) The spelling proficiency was even lower. Out of 12 words given, the participants could spell only 1.10 words correctly. Forty-one participants had spelling scores of zero because they either did not spell any words correctly or were not given the test because of low letter knowledge.

The average performance level on the listening comprehension test was 25%. This low score was due to an interesting effect. In this task, after listening to a passage, the participants answered several questions based on the passage. The general tendency of the participants was to answer these questions based on their own world experiences rather than what the passages had described, even though they were prompted several times to think about what the text said. Hence, because of a lack of formal training, these individuals relied more on their own funds of knowledge (cf. Moll & Greenberg, 1990) rather than on information from a text.

Posttests

On the posttests, the participants showed significant improvements. They could now recognize 51 of the 58 letters (88%) and decode 9 of the 15 short words (62%), 9 of the 12 old words (75%), and 8 of the 12 new words (68%). Their spelling accuracy was 33%. Now all participants took the test, and only 9 participants had a score of zero. Although spelling performance still seems very low considering that there were only nine words in this task, it must be noted that these spelling scores were based on absolute accuracy with no partial credit given. (In the Appendix the actual writing samples of 3 participants are given to highlight the changes in their spelling performance.) No reading comprehension pretest was given because of low word-recognition levels. However after only 90 hr of instruction, the reading comprehension posttest showed that 47% of the comprehension questions were answered correctly.

T tests were conducted on the scores from tests that were repeated before and after the course. (Although spelling and familiar word-recognition tasks were also identical across pre- and postcourse testing, the change in these tasks was not analyzed because of the limited number of participants who completed the task at the beginning of the course.) On letter recognition, there was a significant improvement from 39 letters to 51 letters, $t(58) = 6.25$. There was also a significant improvement in the overall phonological awareness scores, going from 16.56 to 22.14, $t(57) = 5.11$.

Correlations

Table 2 summarizes the correlations among the pretest measures. (Because of the floor effects in overall performance levels, the results from the spelling task need to

TABLE 2
Correlations Among the Pretest Measures

Task	1	2	3	4	5	6	7	8
1. Tapping	1.0	.43*	.59*	.80*	.51*	.62*	.23	.27
2. Blending		1.0	.41*	.74*	.35*	.40*	.23	.35*
3. Deleting			1.0	.87*	.37*	.37*	.34*	.41*
4. Total phonological awareness				1.0	.47*	.55*	.53*	.47*
5. Letter recognition					1.0	.77*	.35*	.23
6. Word recognition						1.0	.37*	.38*
7. Spelling							1.0	.45*
8. Listening comprehension								1.0

*$p < .05$.

be interpreted with caution and are not discussed further.) Several patterns appear in this table. First, not surprisingly, the three phonological awareness tasks were correlated with each other. In the following regression analyses, these tasks were summed into a single score (labeled *total phonological awareness* in the table) to gain more power. Looking at word recognition, it was significantly related to all three phonological awareness measures as well as to their composite. There was also a significant correlation between word recognition and letter knowledge. This pattern is identical to that observed with young children. Letter knowledge and phonological awareness are correlated with word-recognition levels of Turkish beginning readers, too (Durgunoğlu & Öney, 1999; Öney & Durgunoğlu, 1997). Interestingly, unlike the common pattern with children, listening comprehension was related to both word recognition and to two of the phonological awareness measures for the adults. This relation may be mediated by the "school" concept. Those who recognized the most words were also more likely to answer the listening comprehension questions in a decontextualized manner. Therefore, we speculate that a sociocultural factor, rather than a cognitive one, underlies the correlation of listening comprehension with word recognition at the beginning of the course.

Table 3 summarizes the correlations among posttest measures conducted at the end of 90 hr of instruction. As was the case for the pretests, the three phonological awareness measures were correlated, and hence they were summed into a single measure (labeled *total phonological awareness* in the table) for the following regression analyses. Likewise, because the three word-recognition measures (short, old, and new words) were correlated, they were summed into a single word-recognition measure (labeled *total word recognition* in the table). Reading comprehension was strongly related to phonological awareness, word recognition, and spelling as well as to letter recognition.

TABLE 3
Correlations Among the Posttest Measures

Task	1	2	3	4	5	6	7	8	9	10	11
1. Tapping	1.0*										
2. Blending	.32*	1.0									
3. Deleting	.66*	.45*	1.0								
4. Total phonological awareness	.81*	.62*	.94*	1.0							
5. Letter recognition	.54*	.11	.51*	.50*	1.0						
6. Short words	.56*	.46*	.61*	.66*	.50*	1.0					
7. Old words	.51*	.44*	.50*	.56*	.53*	.59*	1.0				
8. New words	.50*	.42*	.42*	.50*	.43*	.52*	.75*	1.0			
9. Total word recognition	.62*	.51*	.61*	.68*	.56*	.86*	.88*	.85*	1.0		
10. Spelling	.49*	.42*	.57*	.63*	.37*	.42*	.50*	.42*	.53*	1.0	
11. Reading comprehension	.68*	.44*	.59*	.69*	.40*	.55*	.44*	.51*	.58*	.40*	1.0

*$p < .05$

257

Multiple Regression Analyses

Several hierarchical multiple regression analyses were conducted to observe progress across time in word recognition, spelling, and reading comprehension. In each analysis, post- and follow-up measures were first regressed on their corresponding measure in the previous testing period to remove the effects of existing performance levels.

At the Beginning of the Course

In the first analysis, we focused on the predictors of the initial word-recognition levels before any instruction had taken place. Although the average word-recognition levels were very low at the beginning of the course (41%), there was great variety in the levels of participants. We predicted that a basic knowledge of letter names can mediate word-recognition performance at the beginning of the course. In Turkish, there are very systematic sound–spelling correspondences. In addition, names of the consonants are their sounds pronounced with /eh/. For example, letter b has the name /beh/, r has the name /reh/, and so on. Therefore, letter names provide reliable clues as to how the letters are pronounced in a written word.

In this multiple regression analysis, the predictors of precourse word recognition were entered in the following order: precourse listening comprehension, precourse phonological awareness, and precourse letter recognition to investigate if letter knowledge is significant even after the effects of listening comprehension and phonological awareness are considered.

This analysis (see Table 4) indicated that a participant's initial listening comprehension, phonological awareness, and letter recognition levels at the beginning of the course predicted 65% of the variance in the initial word-recognition levels. In the final equation, the only significant predictor was the existing letter-recognition level, explaining 33% of the variance even after listening comprehension and phonological awareness were entered into the equation.

TABLE 4
Predictors of Existing Word-Recognition Knowledge at the Beginning of the Course

	Precourse Word Recognition	
Step	R^2 Explained	β
Precourse listening comprehension	14.8%	.167
Precourse phonological awareness	+17.7%	.151
Precourse letter recognition	+32.8%	.657*
Total variance explained	65.3%	

*$p < .05$.

At the End of the Course

As summarized at the top of Table 5, development of postcourse word recognition and spelling levels were also analyzed using multiple regression. For each equation, we first entered the pretest levels of the corresponding test, followed by postcourse phonological awareness and postcourse letter knowledge. The rationale was that once the preexisting levels of a task were considered, it was more important to use the data from predictors that existed at the end of the course, reflecting development. Because letter recognition was a strong predictor in pretest analyses, it was entered last to see if it explained any additional variance once the preexisting levels and phonological awareness performance were entered into the equation.

For word recognition, all three predictors (precourse word recognition, postcourse phonological awareness, and postcourse letter recognition) were significant and together explained 57% of the variance. For spelling, precourse spelling level and postcourse phonological awareness level were the significant predictors, together explaining 45% of the variance. It must be noted that for both spelling and word recognition, even after the precourse levels were taken into consideration, the developing phonological awareness still played an important role. In spelling performance, letter recognition did not add any explanatory power once phonological awareness was included. However, in word recognition, letter knowledge was still significant even after phonological awareness was entered into the equation.

TABLE 5
Predictors of the Outcome Measures at the End of the Course

Step	Postcourse Spelling		Postcourse Word Recognition	
	R^2 Explained	β	R^2 Explained	β
Precourse word recognition			41.0%	.320*
Precourse spelling	+20.2%	.229**		
Postcourse phonological awareness	+24.4%	.511*	+12.6%	.370**
Postcourse letter recognition	+0.3%	.061	+3.2	.214**
Total variance explained	44.9%		56.8%	

	Postcourse Reading Comprehension	
	R^2	β
Precourse listening comprehension	18.6%	.125
Postcourse phonological awareness	+29.4%	.471**
Postcourse letter recognition	+0.2%	−.012
Postcourse word recognition	+2.6%	.232*
Total variance explained	50.8%	

$*p < .09.$ $**p < .05.$

In analyzing reading comprehension performance at the end of the course (see the bottom portion of Table 5), listening comprehension (measured before the course) was entered first because reading comprehension could not be assessed in the beginning. Phonological awareness and letter-recognition levels at the end of the course were entered in the next two steps to make this analysis parallel to those of word recognition and spelling performances given at the top of Table 5. However, for reading comprehension, word recognition was also added as a fourth variable to measure any effects of decoding processes (such as recognizing larger orthographic units) above and beyond those explained by phonological awareness and letter recognition. Overall, the four variables explained 51% of the variance, and, interestingly, the only significant predictor was phonological awareness. (Word recognition was a marginally significant predictor.) For adults, after a 3-month period of literacy instruction, phonological awareness was still a strong predictor of reading comprehension. In Turkish children, after 1 year of instruction, phonological awareness loses its predictive power because it influences reading comprehension indirectly through word recognition (Öney & Durgunoğlu, 1997). In these adult participants, though, the power of phonological awareness was still very strong, possibly because of the shorter time frame of this study.

GENERAL DISCUSSION

The goal of this research was to observe the cognitive processes in Turkish adult literacy acquisition and to highlight any similarities and differences as compared to general models of child literacy acquisition. Because most literacy models are based on English-speaking children, in this study there are two possible sources of variation that are addressed separately. The first issue is child literacy acquisition in Turkish and how it compares with child literacy acquisition in English. The second issue is how Turkish adult literacy acquisition compares with Turkish child literacy acquisition.

As we discussed elsewhere (Durgunoğlu & Öney, 1999; Öney & Durgunoğlu, 1997; Öney & Goldman, 1984), the characteristics of a language can impact the child literacy acquisition patterns. Turkish, with its very systematic spelling–sound correspondences, facilitates word-recognition and spelling performances, despite literacy instruction that does not make these links explicit. On the other hand, the complex morphological structure leads to long, multisyllabic words that provide a challenge. However, the well-marked syllable boundaries that override the morphemic boundaries provide a big source of help. Finally, the vowel harmony that changes the nature of inflections (e.g., *ler* or *lar* for pluralization, depending on the preceding vowel) forces the children to notice these phonemic changes in their oral language. As a result, both syllable and phoneme awareness develop rapidly. However, the facilitatory effects of phonological awareness on word recognition and spelling are briefer compared to English-speaking children. As decoding proficiency develops quickly because of the transparent orthography, the impact of phonological awareness is reduced. Also, for Turkish children, low listening comprehension is a more serious bottleneck in reading comprehension rather than the decoding skills that hinder reading comprehension of English-speaking children. In short, there are parallels in Turkish and English literacy acquisition of children. For both languages, variables such as letter recognition, phonological awareness, and listening comprehension (the building blocks discussed in the introduction) affect literacy acquisition. However, the pace of development, impact, and the duration of these factors are language specific.

A second question is how adult and child literacy acquisition in Turkish compare. It is clear that this comparison has several limitations. First, the children in our previous studies and the adult participants of FALP in this study have different instructional backgrounds. FALP participants were tested after 90 hr of instruction whereas children were tested after 1 year of instruction. In addition, FALP has a different educational philosophy, making spelling–sound correspondences the starting point of literacy instruction, unlike what is found in the elementary schools. Of course, our child and adult participants have sociocultural differences and life histories that also make them quite different from each other. Finally, we cannot judge how equivalent the adults in this study are to the children in our previous studies in terms of reading comprehension. Although we cannot compare the absolute levels of performance between adults and children, the patterns of the literacy acquisition predictors show similarities.

In this study with adults, the participants started the courses with very low levels of literacy proficiencies. After only 90 hr of instruction, there were significant improvements in their letter and word recognition, spelling, phonological awareness, and reading comprehension levels. The transparent orthography, as well as the course making this characteristic explicit, enabled the adult participants to develop decoding proficiencies quickly (although not perfectly). Further evidence for this is found in another study in which we compared the FALP participants with the participants of the classical adult literacy courses that used the holistic method similar to the instruction in the elementary schools. FALP participants who received explicit letter, sound, and syllable instruction showed more significant gains in word-recognition and spelling performance (Durgunoğlu et al., 2002). However, although word recognition progressed rapidly with 90 hr of FALP instruction, the duration of the course was too short for reading comprehension and spelling to become fully established. Currently, we have extended the duration of FALP to 120 hr and developed another 90-hr course (FALP2) to make the program more compatible with the 200- to 300-hr programs found elsewhere around the world (Comings, 1995).

As for the predictors and facilitators of adult and child literacy acquisition, word-recognition proficiency was significantly related to both letter recognition and phonological awareness, replicating the pattern reported in numerous studies of child literacy acquisition in English. In addition, this study replicated child literacy studies in Turkish (Durgunoğlu & Öney, 1999; Öney & Durgunoğlu, 1997), drawing intralinguistic parallels between adult and child literacy acquisition.

One difference between child and adult studies was the longer lasting influence of phonological awareness in the adult data. This, of course, may be due to the relatively short period (90 hr) of instruction. Because both word recognition and reading comprehension still had room for improvement, the influence of phonological awareness was continuing. To summarize, the results of this longitudinal study showed that literacy acquisition progresses in remarkably similar ways in children and adults, at least in the context of Turkish.

ACKNOWLEDGMENTS

Preparation of this manuscript was partly supported by the Spencer Foundation.

We thank Hilal Kuscul, Fatma Zengin, and Meltem Cantürk for their help in data collection and collation and the Mother Child Education Foundation for its continuous support.

REFERENCES

Abadzi, H. (1995, April). *Difficulties of adults in the acquisition of reading skills: A review of evidence.* Paper presented at the American Educational Research Association, San Francisco, CA.

Adams, M. J. (1990). *Beginning to read: Thinking and learning about print.* Cambridge, MA: MIT Press.

Aksu-Koc, A., & Slobin, D. I. (1986). The acquisition of Turkish. In D. I. Slobin (Ed.), *The crosslinguistic study of language acquisition* (Vol. 1, pp. 839–878). Hillsdale, NJ: Lawrence Erlbaum Associates, Inc.

Arnove, R. F., & Graff, H. J. (1987). Introduction. In R. F. Arnove & H. J. Graff (Eds.), *National literacy campaigns* (pp. 1–28). New York: Plenum.

Ball, E. W., & Blachman, B. A. (1991). Does phoneme awareness in kindergarten make a difference in early word recognition and developmental spelling? *Reading Research Quarterly, 26,* 49–66.

Ballara, M. (1992). *Women and literacy.* London: Zed Books.

Chall, J. (1987). Reading development in adults. *Annals of Dyslexia, 37,* 240–251.

Comings, J. (1995). Literacy skill retention in adult students in developing countries. *International Journal of Educational Development, 15,* 37–45.

Cunningham, A. E., & Stanovich, K. E. (1991). Tracking the unique effects of print exposure: Associations with vocabulary, general knowledge, and spelling. *Journal of Educational Psychology, 83,* 264–274.

Curtis, M. E. (1980). Development of components of reading skill. *Journal of Educational Psychology, 72,* 656–669.

Durgunoğlu, A. Y. (2000). *Adult literacy: Issues of personal and community development.* Final report to the Spencer Foundation, Author.

Durgunoğlu, A. Y. (2001, November). *Linguistic properties of Turkish and their implication for literacy development.* Paper presented at the NATO–Advanced Study Institute, Il Ciocco, Italy.

Durgunoğlu, A. Y. (in press). Reading morphologically complex words in Turkish. In E. Assink & D. Sandra (Eds.), *Reading complex words.* Dordrecht, The Netherlands: Kluwer.

Durgunoğlu, A. Y., Nagy, W. E., & Hancin-Bhatt, B. J. (1993). Cross-language transfer of phonological awareness. *Journal of Educational Psychology, 85,* 453–465.

Durgunoğlu, A., & Öney, B. (1999). A cross linguistic comparison of phonological awareness and word recognition. *Reading and Writing, 11,* 281–299.

Durgunoğlu, A. Y., Öney, B., & Kuscul, H. (1995, April). *Evaluation of a functional adult literacy program in Istanbul, Turkey.* Paper presented at the American Educational Research Association, San Francisco, CA.

Durgunoğlu, A., Öney, B., & Kuscul, H. (2002). Development and evaluation of an adult literacy program in Turkey. *International Journal of Educational Development.*

Gillette, A. (1987). The experimental world literacy program. In R. F. Arnove & H. J. Graff (Eds.), *National literacy campaigns* (pp. 197–217). New York: Plenum.

Goswami, U., & Bryant, P. (1990). *Phonological skills and learning to read.* East Sussex, UK: Lawrence Erlbaum Associates, Inc.

Gough, P. B., & Tunmer, W. E. (1986). Decoding, reading, and reading disability. *Remedial and Special Education, 7,* 6–10.

Greaney, V. (1996). *Promoting reading in developing countries.* Newark, DE: International Reading Association.

Greenberg, D., Ehri, L. C., & Perin, D. (1997). Are word-reading processes the same or different in adult literacy students and third–fifth graders matched for reading level? *Journal of Educational Psychology, 89,* 262–275.

Hoover, W. A., & Tunmer, W. E. (1993). The components of reading. In G. B. Thompson, W. E. Tunmer, & T. Nicholson (Eds.), *Reading acquisition processes* (pp. 1–19). Philadelphia: Multilingual Matters.

Juel, C., Griffith, P. L., & Gough, P. B. (1986). Acquisition of literacy: A longitudinal study of children in first and second grade. *Journal of Educational Psychology, 78,* 243–255.

Kirsch, I. (1993). *Adult literacy in America: A first look at the results of the National Adult Literacy Survey.* Washington, DC. (ERIC Document Reproduction Service No. ED3583375)

Liberman, A. M. (1989). Reading is hard just because listening is easy. In C. V. Euler, I. Lundberg, & G. Lennerstrand (Eds.), *Brain and reading* (pp. 197–206). London: Macmillan.

Lukatela, K., Carello, C., Shankweiler, D., & Liberman, I. Y. (1995). Phonological awareness in illiterates: Observations from Serbo-Croatian. *Applied Psycholinguistics, 16,* 463–487.

Maclean, M., Bryant, P., & Bradley, L. (1988). Rhymes, nursery rhymes and reading in early childhood. In K. Stanovich (Ed.), *Children's reading and the development of phonological awareness* (pp. 11–37). Detroit: Wayne State University Press.

Moll, L. C., & Greenberg, J. (1990). Creating zones of possibilities: Combining social contexts for instruction. In L. C. Moll (Ed.), *Vygotsky and education* (pp. 319–348). Cambridge, England: Cambridge University Press.

Morais, J., Cary, L., Alegria, J., & Bertelson, P. (1979). Does awareness of speech as a sequence of phones arise spontaneously? *Cognition, 7,* 4323–4331.

Morais, J., Content, A., Bertelson, P., & Cary, L. (1988). Is there a critical period for the acquisition of segmental analysis? *Cognitive Neuropsychology, 5,* 347–352.

Oakhill, J. (1994). Individual differences in children's text comprehension. In M. A. Gernsbacher (Ed.), *Handbook of psycholinguistics* (pp. 821–848). San Diego: Academic.

Öney, B., & Durgunoğlu, A. Y. (1997). Beginning to read in Turkish: A phonologically transparent orthography. *Applied Psycholinguistics, 18,* 1–15.

Öney, B., & Goldman, S. R. (1984). Decoding and comprehension skills in Turkish and English: Effects of the regularity of grapheme–phoneme correspondences. *Journal of Educational Psychology, 76,* 557–568.

Perfetti, C., & Marron, M. (1995). *Literacy acquisition by children and adults* (Tech. Rep.). Philadelphia: National Center on Adult Literacy.

Perin, D. (1988). Combining schema activation and cooperative learning to promote reading comprehension in adult literacy students. *Journal of Reading, 32,* 54–68.

Pratt, A. C., & Brady, S. (1988). Relation of phonological awareness to reading disability in children and adults. *Journal of Educational Psychology, 80,* 319–323.

Ramdas, L. (1989). Women and literacy: A quest for justice. *Prospects, 19,* 519–530.

Sabatini, J. (1999). Adult reading acquisition. In D. Wagner, R. L. Venezky, & B. Street (Eds.), *Literacy: An international handbook* (pp. 49–53). Boulder, CO: Westview.

Salthouse, T. A. (1994). The nature of the influence of speed on adult age differences in cognition. *Developmental Psychology, 30,* 240–259.

Shankweiler, D. (1989). How problems of comprehension are related to difficulties in decoding. In I. Y. Liberman & D. Shankweiler (Eds.), *Phonology and reading disability: Solving the reading puzzle* (pp. 1–33). Ann Arbor: University of Michigan Press.

Stanovich, K. E., & Cunningham, A. E. (1993). Where does knowledge come from? Specific associations between print exposure and information acquisition. *Journal of Educational Psychology, 85,* 211–229.

Treiman, R. (1991). Phonological awareness and its roles in learning to read and spell. In D. J. Sawyer & B. J. Fox (Eds.), *Phonological awareness and reading: The evolution of current perspective* (pp. 159–189). New York: Springer-Verlag.

Vellutino, F. R., & Scanlon, D. M. (1988). Phonological coding, phonological awareness, and reading ability: Evidence from a longitudinal and experimental study. In K. E. Stanovich (Ed.), *Children's reading and development of phonological awareness* (pp. 77–119). Detroit, MI: Wayne State University Press.

Wimmer, H., Landerl, K., Linortner, R., & Hummer, P. (1991). The relationship of phonemic awareness to reading acquisition: More consequence than precondition, but still important. *Cognition, 40,* 219–249.

Manuscript received July 27, 2001
Final revision received December 1, 2001
Accepted December 4, 2001

APPENDIX

Words on the test:
göl terlik fincan savaş tabakalara yıllardan sümbül kaslarımızın kamyonlar

Pre- and post-course spelling samples of three participants

Participant 87

pretest   posttest

ou

göl

terlik

fecan

savaş

tobakalara

yıtadan

sebul

kaslarızım

kayolar

Participant 75

pretest   posttest

gi   Svş rii rprif

                    gol Fican Savaş Teik

                    Tabakalara yiladon sübü!

                    kaSrahimiz kamiyolar

participant 136

pretest   posttest

                    göl   Fiçan Savaş Terlik
öll
Ysan   Tabakalara Yildan Sübul
Savaş
                    Koslaribiz Kamaynlar
TFRi

TaBakai

YI DI

SCIENTIFIC STUDIES OF READING, 6(3), 267–298
Copyright © 2002, Lawrence Erlbaum Associates, Inc.

Efficiency in Word Reading of Adults: Ability Group Comparisons

John P. Sabatini

National Center on Adult Literacy
University of Pennsylvania

Whereas the fundamental relation of phonological skills to early reading acquisition has been firmly established, research on the relation of speed/rate to the acquisition of decoding and reading fluency are works in progress. This study addresses the question of the role of general speed/rate of processing in reading impairment in adults. Ninety-five adults varying in word-recognition ability were divided into subgroups, and their scores on basic speed, decoding, and comprehension component skill tasks were compared. Results showed significant and pervasive speed/rate differences among groups, as well as differences in accuracy of performance. The results are interpreted in terms of theories of speed of processing as a basic capacity and of complexity–capacity interactions.

Although considerable progress has been made in understanding the causal relation of phonological processes to normal word reading acquisition and disabilities (Share & Stanovich, 1995), understanding the role of processing speed, often indexed by naming-speed measures, has been somewhat more elusive (Abadzi, 1996; Bowers & Wolf, 1993; Carver, 1997; Carver & David, 2001; Farmer & Klein, 1995; Manis, Seidenberg, & Doi, 1999; Stringer & Stanovich, 2000; Wimmer, Mayringer, & Landerl, 1998; Wolf, 1991, 1997; Wolf & Bowers, 2000). A main focus of inquiry and theorizing has been on understanding the empirical relation between rapid automatized naming (RAN) and reading disability (Booth, Perfetti, MacWhinney, & Hunt, 2000; Bowers, Sunseth, & Golden, 1999; Denckla & Rudel, 1976; Farmer & Klein, 1995; Klein & Farmer, 1995; Rayner, Pollatsek, & Bilsky, 1995; Studdert-Kennedy & Mody, 1995; Tallal, Miller, Jenkins, & Merzenich, 1997; Torgesen, 1997; Wolf & Bowers, 1999; Wolf, Bowers, & Biddle, 2000).

Requests for reprints should be sent to John P. Sabatini, National Center on Adult Literacy, University of Pennsylvania, 3910 Chestnut Street, Philadelphia, PA 19104.

Three questions have been central: (a) Is RAN a distinct measure of independent, reading-related cognitive skills or simply another measure of phonological skill; (b) what are the underlying determinants of the RAN tasks most responsible for the breakdown of reading in dyslexia; and (c) is the RAN indicative of a broader cognitive processing speed problem?

For the first question, an extensive literature now demonstrates the independence of the two measures. In their conceptual review, Wolf et al. (2000), although acknowledging that RAN tasks have shared variance with phonological skills and involve accessing phonological codes, nonetheless, pointed to important aspects of timing within and across the complex cognitive subprocesses that comprise naming tasks that go beyond the constructs measuring phonological skills. They cited evidence for RAN tasks independent predictive relations to other reading subskills. In general, phonological skills are most predictive of decoding in reading, and naming-speed tasks are most predictive of fluency (Manis et al., 1999; Wolf & Katzir-Cohen, 2001).

For the second question, one reason for the difficulty in precisely specifying the nature of rapid naming effects in reading disabilities stems from the multicomponential nature of the underlying components in RAN tasks. Naming involves attention, visual recognition, and access to phonological codes, articulation, and temporal processing—all important for normal reading development. A considerable body of evidence identifies naming-speed deficits in disabled readers, which, when combined with phonological deficits, creates what Wolf and Bowers characterized as a double-deficit subtype of dyslexia (Wolf, 1997; Wolf & Bowers, 1999).

The third question, and the focus of this article, concerns general speed/rate of processing in reading impairment as contrasted with domain-specific factors such as naming-speed deficits that are common to dyslexia. Developmental improvement in processing speed can be described well by an exponential function, which "captures the fact that processing speed shows initially rapid and then progressively more gradual improvements throughout childhood and into adolescence" (Fry & Hale, 2000, p. 5). From ages of approximately 6 to 12 years, general processing speed shows a steep increase of 5 SDs, based on the variance in processing speeds of 18-year-olds. From ages 12 to 18, speed increases 1 SD. General speed of processing reaches a plateau for most individuals in young adulthood (age 18) and remains at this plateau until the age of 35. It then declines steadily across the remainder of the lifespan (Kail & Salthouse, 1994). The construct of general processing speed is derived from a variety of measures including motor–perceptual tasks, intelligence test subtests that load on speed, and naming tasks (Fry & Hale, 2000; Salthouse, 1991). Thus, it is difficult to disassociate increases in specific speeded processes as children learn a skill from the more general phenomenon of developmental changes in global processing speed.

SPEED OF PROCESSING AS A BASIC CAPACITY

Developmental changes in general processing speed play an important role in the development of many component processes involved in normal reading acquisition. Fry and Hale (2000), for example, reviewed the relations among cognitive processing speed, working memory (Gathercole & Baddeley, 1993), and fluid intelligence. They concluded, first, that all three follow similar developmental time courses and, second, that processing speed appears to mediate age-related changes in working memory and fluid intelligence improvement. Specifically, Fry and Hale (1996) found that almost half of age-related increase in fluid intelligence (as measured by Ravens Progressive Matrices) was mediated by developmental changes in processing speed and that three fourths of working memory improvement was mediated by processing speed. Furthermore, individual differences in processing speed had a direct effect on working memory capacity, even when other measures were controlled, which, in turn, was a direct determinant of fluid intelligence. The reverse causality prediction—that differences in fluid intelligence accounted for changes in processing speed or working memory—was not upheld.[1]

This finding supports the theory that general processing speed is a basic capacity that mediates acquisition of articulation time, working memory, and some aspects of higher order processing (Kail & Hall, 1994; Kail & Park, 1994; Kail & Salthouse, 1994). The theory of general processing speed as a basic mental capacity has also been used to account for the differential effects of speed on learning (Kail & Hall, 1994; Kail, Hall, & Caskey, 1999; Kail & Salthouse, 1994; Salthouse, 1991, 1992). This aspect of the theory posits that general processing speed is a basic mental capacity that mediates cognitive performance in two ways: directly, because of its influence on basic cognitive resources, such as allocating attention to different processes, and indirectly, by influencing skill-specific learning processes. The direct route hypothesis is supported by evidence such as the association between word length and size of working memory span (Gathercole & Baddeley, 1993). Lengthy items take more time to articulate, both subvocally and overtly. Consequently, decay rates are found to be more rapid for lengthier items.

The Kail and colleagues studies provided evidence supporting a relation between general processing speed and acquisition of reading skills in normally developing children and adolescents. The National Reading Panel (2000) finding that interventions not initiated early in a child's schooling have had more limited success in remediating reading is suggestive of factors in addition to phonological

---

[1]The Fry and Hale theory has implications for modeling cause or consequence in reading development. For example, controlling for nonverbal IQ (using Raven's Matrices) by entering it as a covariate or as a first step in a regression model has the effect of reducing the variance attributable to processing speed and working memory variables. If one theorizes that speed of processing is a more basic determinant, one would not want to attribute its predictive variance to more distal measures.

processing difficulties in reading acquisition. Interactions of processing speed on reading skill acquisition and fluency is one such potential factor.

STUDYING WORD RECOGNITION IN
LOW-LITERATE ADULTS

General processing speed differences and limits could have important implications for low-literate adults reading ability and acquisition. For example, limited or slow processing could exacerbate individual differences whenever task complexity increases, regardless of or in addition to core phonological processing problems (Just & Carpenter, 1992; Perfetti, 1985). In the most extreme cases (i.e., readers with dyslexia), a more severe speed deficit may manifest itself as a deficit of its own or a double-deficit, qualitatively changing the nature of processing at the most fundamental levels (e.g., Farmer & Klein, 1995; Tallal et al., 1997; Wolf & Bowers, 1999). However, in less severe cases, basic speed may still interact with the quantity and quality of instruction and practice to influence word-recognition skill acquisition. That is, the slower rate of learning would require significantly more practice to consolidate subcomponent skills.

In this article we look at patterns of subskill processing in groups of adults at different ability levels across a range of component tasks to better understand what kinds of processing underlie their different ability profiles. We focus attention on groups scoring within 1 *SD* below the mean for college-level ability in word-recognition skill. These are poor readers who would be difficult to classify categorically as dyslexic when using common diagnostic approaches (Fowler & Scarborough, 1993). We explore the continuum of processing difficulties across the range from the most severely disabled to efficient, high-ability readers to highlight the pervasive processing speed differences that are correlated with this achievement gap.

Studies of adults who are poor readers or readers with dyslexia consistently report deficiencies in decoding and word-recognition skills, with reading comprehension performance more variable (Bell & Perfetti, 1994; Bruck, 1990; Byrne & Ledez, 1983; Fowler & Scarborough, 1993; Greenberg, Ehri, & Perin, 1997; Pennington, Van Orden, Smith, Green, & Haith, 1990; Pratt & Brady, 1988; Read & Ruyter, 1985; Ross-Gordon, 1998; Share & Stanovich, 1995). The literature on relatively successful disabled adult readers also shows persistent deficits in processing speed on a variety of reading tasks (e.g., Abadzi, 1996; Fink, 1998; Fowler & Scarborough, 1993).

The low-literate adults in this study differ from other samples in three respects. First, this sample was distributed across reading abilities from intermediate beginners (about third-grade-equivalent ability) through college level. The distributions of narrower age and grade ranges are truncated, weakening the relation between a predictor and outcome variable. This wider range allows us to examine patterns across intermediate groups between high and low ability, for example, exploring whether variables are relatively stronger predictors across specific ranges of the distribution. Second, differences in adult processing speeds are relatively stable reflections of individual differences, or they reflect the degree of learning and practice in specific domains. Cross-age speed comparisons with children become more complex because each year of age produces significant increases in basic cognitive processing speed due to maturation, as well as domain-specific increases in speed due to experience and knowledge (Kail & Salthouse, 1994).

Third, samples of adults in literacy classes differ from samples identified based on clinical adult dyslexia criteria. Studies of adults with dyslexia typically select individuals with normal to high verbal IQ; normal math achievement; mainstream social and educational background; an absence of other cognitive, emotional, or sensory problems; and often a history of formal and informal attempts at compensating for their specific reading disability (Fowler & Scarborough, 1993). Consequently, many of the adults with dyslexia studied have achieved a relatively high level of educational achievement, such as reading comprehension at the college level. Repeated attempts at compensation influence certain variables (e.g., a relative advantage in orthographic processing, wider exposure to texts, and growth or maintenance of age-appropriate verbal IQ). In fact, persistently poor performance on basic phonological processing tasks (such as pseudoword decoding) despite repeated attempts at remediation is one of the strongest pieces of evidence of the fundamental role of phonological processing in dyslexia.

Adults attending literacy classes, on the other hand, typically have significantly less educational attainment and experience. They are predominantly high school dropouts or social promotion graduates from low socioeconomic status communities. The main interpretive difference we infer is that they have not had as much educational compensation and support as other dyslexic groups studied. Because these low-literate adults have less compensatory experience, models of reading processes from the adult dyslexic literature may or may not generalize to them (Bruck, 1990; Fowler & Scarborough, 1993).

RESEARCH QUESTIONS

The study examines how comprehension, decoding, and basic speed of processing tasks vary across word-recognition-ability groups. Three main research questions are addressed. First, are there significant group differences among ability groups on processing task measures, and, if so, how do group differences vary with respect to speed/rate versus accuracy? Second, are differences in accuracy or speed a function of task complexity? Based on our reading of the Just and Carpenter (1992) model, which demonstrated how working memory is overloaded as complexity increases, our prediction is that processing speed will be highly correlated with complexity, such that slower processors will experience nonlinear difficulty for each added component of task or stimulus complexity. By contrast, high-speed, efficient processors will show minimal difference in speed or accuracy of performance across a wider range of task or stimulus complexities. The third question asks, What are the similarities and differences in profiles of component skills of high-, average-, and low-ability groups of adults? What are the parameters of efficient component reading processes in terms of speed and accuracy? Is decoding ability sometimes slow, effortful, but accurate? At what levels are decoding skills generally slow, effortful, and inaccurate? Are there patterns that typify transitional states?

METHOD

Data from 95 participants (ages 16–53) were analyzed in this study. Fifty-two adult literacy learners were recruited from adult education programs in the mid-Atlantic region, including correctional institution educational classes, community-based programs, adult basic education classes, general educational development classes, public assistance job programs, and tutoring services.[2] This group was 63% male, 54% White, 40% African American, and 6% other. Twelve percent had educational levels of 8 years or less, 65% had between 9 and 12 years, and 18% had a general education development or high school diploma. Thirty-eight percent self-reported some learning problems during their formal school years, although this was not significantly correlated with the outcome measures. All participants were fluent English speakers, however, 6 participants were non-U.S. born and had some of their education in their countries of origin. Participants were judged by teachers and staff to be in the normal range of IQ, but no intelligence tests were administered. All testing was done at instructional sites by the project staff and the author.

A total of 42 college-level learners (ages 18–52) were recruited. Twenty-nine were volunteers taking an undergraduate study skills class; another 13 were continuing education students who responded to study recruitment announcements. The group was 37% male, 86% White, 5% African American, and 9% other. All

---

[2]The subsample of adult literacy learners was drawn from a larger sample of 102 adult learners who participated in a longitudinal research project designed to measure the development of component reading skills of adults enrolled in instructional programs. All participants were recruited by project staff with the support of instructors and were paid $50 for participating. The full test battery was administered across multiple sessions. Of the 102 participants who completed the initial battery, 52 completed the full battery. The subsample of 52 was similar to the full group in demographics including age, gender, ethnicity, educational levels, and self-report of learning problems in school.

had some college-level education. Nineteen percent reported that they received help for a learning problem while in school; one was undergoing testing at the time of the study. Three of those who identified themselves as having learning problems were subsequently identified as outlying cases based on the distance of some of their component reading scores from the distribution plots of the other skilled readers; however, they were not outliers with respect to the full sample. All participants were fluent English speakers; however, 2 participants were non-U.S. born and had some of their education in their countries of origin. All testing was done at a university lab site.

Standard scores were used in forming word-recognition-ability groups. The Wide Range Achievement Test (WRAT; Jastak & Associates, 1993) manual uses standard score ranges to characterize word-recognition ability from *deficient* through *very superior*. Using these WRAT classification levels, seven ability groups were formed: superior (120 and above; $n = 7$); high average (110–119; $n = 18$; hereafter high), average (90–109; $n = 37$), low average (80–89; $n = 19$; hereafter low), borderline (70–79; $n = 9$), and deficient (below 70, $n = 5$). Because the average group covered a 20-point span, we divided it into two subgroups: avg100 (100–109) and avg90 (90–99).

The four midrange ability groups (high, avg100, avg90, and low) were used to conduct analyses. They are spaced in 10-point steps around the mean of 100 on the WRAT (approximately 12th-grade word-recognition ability[3]), for a final sample size of 73. Ten points represents about two thirds *SD* and a little over two standard errors of measurement. The superior group in our sample and two lowest ability groups (hereafter very low) were eliminated from statistical analyses because small sizes may have biased the significance tests.[4] The means for these groups appear in the tables and charts, however, because they are of interest in understanding the overall patterns of readers. The very low group may be of special interest to some because these readers are 2 full *SD*s below the mean and represent the traditionally defined disabled reader.

---

[3]I chose to use only the standard scores from the norm range for 17- to 19-year-olds as a reference. Using age-appropriate standard scores lowers the scores for the older learners, increasing the strength of the negative correlation between age and WRAT because the low-literate learners do not get any better with age. Because many low-literate adults have had limited postschool reading experience, the fixed WRAT norm level was more appropriate. I have run all the analyses using age-appropriate standard scores. The results and conclusions for the five groups of approximate equal size (now including a borderline group, $n = 16$) are consistent with those reported in the main Results section.

[4]Initial analyses run either with the borderline group only or with a combined borderline/deficient group did find significant differences in the main effect and in most post hoc tests between these very low ability groups as compared to the other subgroups. However, there is an increased chance of Type I error rate and an inflated alpha level when the smallest group has the largest variance (Tabachnick & Fidell, 1989). The data are consistent with there being a significant difference, but the cautions regarding inflated Type I error hold.

INSTRUMENTS[5]

Word-Recognition Ability

Wide Range Achievement Test–Reading (WRAT–R) subtest. The WRAT–R (Jastak & Associates, 1993) is a word-recognition test that consists of naming 15 letters and 38 words. Scoring is based on accurate pronunciations, including unusual pronunciations due to colloquialisms, foreign accents, or defective articulation.

Comprehension

Wechsler Individual Achievement Test (WIAT) Reading Comprehension subtest. The WIAT (Psychological Corporation, 1990) reading comprehension subtest consists of short passages followed by free response questions. The learner reads a passage at his or her own rate and answers a single question read aloud by a trained administrator. Responses are given orally. The 38-item test takes between 10 and 20 min to administer.

Sentence processing task. In the sentence processing task, participants see a simple line picture (e.g., a triangle over a square) and 2 sec later see a sentence centered below the picture. Thirty-two picture–sentence pairs were constructed to differ systematically on two dichotomous dimensions: affirmative–negative sentence form (e.g., The square is in the triangle./The square is not in the triangle.) and true–false relation between sentence and picture. There are various relations described (e.g., over, under, inside of, between) in random order with half true, half false, half affirmative, and half negative. Measures of both accuracy and response time were collected. (See Clark & Chase, 1972, for review of this paradigm in the psychological literature.)

Decoding

Word and pseudoword naming. The word naming task consists of thirty 1-, 2-, or 3-syllable words covering a span of printed word frequency bands based

---

[5]Reliability coefficients for the component tasks designed for the study, including parallel test forms, were computed based on the repeated tests sessions completed by the full adult literacy group ($n = 102$) using Kuder-Richardson 21, Cronbach's alpha, and split-half test–retest coefficients as appropriate. Coefficients across the tasks ranged from .89 to .94, including sentence, decoding, and word-recognition tasks. Other measures not reported here included vision and auditory screening, vocabulary knowledge, a listening version of the sentence task, silent reading rate, and a think-aloud decoding task. See Sabatini (1997) and Sabatini, Venezky, Jain, and Kharik (2000) for a full description of measures, reliability coefficients, and validity analyses.

on Kucera and Francis (1967). The pseudoword naming task consists of two 24-item blocks of 2- to 5-letter pseudowords. The two blocks are random reordering of the 24 items, thus each item is named two times by each participant. Accuracy and voice onset times were the main measures. Responses were audio recorded to score for accuracy.

Lexical decision decoding tasks.   In addition to pseudoword naming, two other lexical decision-style decoding tasks were administered. In the paired-word task, participants see pairs of made up words, one of which sounds like an English word (pseudohomophone) but is spelled differently. They must choose the word that sounds most like an English word. One of two parallel, 30-item forms was administered. In the single-word task, participants see a single made-up word and are asked to decide whether it sounds like an English word. One of two parallel forms, consisting of three blocks of 40 items each, was administered. The three blocks are random reordering of the 40 items, thus each item is seen three times by each participant. Measures of both accuracy and response time were collected.

Basic Speed Measures

Digit and picture naming.   Digit naming consists of 10 single-digit Arabic numerals repeated twice in random order. Picture naming consists of 11 line drawings of well-known objects (e.g., pencil, elephant) repeated twice in random order. Items are presented individually and voice onset times were collected. Responses were also audio recorded to check accuracy.

Perceptual–motor reaction time (PERC–RT).   The tasks just described use voice onset time as the primary measure of response rate. To test whether slow response time was a general characteristic of the individual (evidenced by slow voice onset time and slow motor reaction time), a composite variable was constructed. The variable consisted of the average response time of correct practice trials used to acclimate the participant to the keypad choices in the decision-style tasks. Participants had 10 practice trials for each of the three decision tasks.

Rapid number naming (RNN).   The New York Optometric Association's K-D Eye Tracking Test (Bernell Corporation, n.d.) was given. The RNN consists of three cards of 40 (eight rows of five digits each) single-digit Arabic numerals in random order. The numbers are not evenly spaced, requiring one to track the digits with one's eyes (which distinguishes this test from other RAN measures that use regularly spaced stimuli). On Card 1, a solid line connects the horizontal numbers, with ¾-in. row spacing. On Card 2, there are no horizontal lines, and on Card 3 the row spacing is reduced to ½ in. Normative mean differences (with standard deviations in parentheses) for the oldest age given (14-year-olds) for each card are 372 (60), 422 (58), and 468 (62) msec/digit, respectively. Total time reading each card was summed and transformed into digits/msec to make comparable with other naming rate metrics.

PROCEDURE

The computer-administered tests (basic speed, decoding, and sentence tasks) were programmed for use on Macintosh® LC 575s with 12-in. screens. All instructions, demonstration trials, practice trials, and test items were delivered by computer. The administrator observed and answered participant questions as necessary.

The items used in the component skill tasks were designed to be of low difficulty for skilled readers, so as to be more reliable estimators of response rates. This decision led to ceiling effects on several tests for the high-skilled participants. Response times were calculated using mean response speed for items answered correctly. Items more than 2 *SD* from an individual's mean response speed were eliminated.

RESULTS

Skill Group Differences by Task

Table 1 shows means and standard deviations for all measures and Table 2 shows correlations. An analysis of variance (ANOVA) using SAS general linear model for unequal size groups was run to make multiple comparisons with skill group as the between-subjects factor. Post hoc, unplanned comparisons using the Scheffé method were used to identify how groups differ from each other. In all of the analyses, response rates (the inverse of speed) were used. The inverse transformation increased normality, reduced the uneven variances across groups, and improved linearity. The inverse functions can be interpreted to mean that smaller differences at higher speeds are similar to larger differences at slower speeds. Millisecond differences (with standard deviations in parentheses) of 455–500 (45), 555–625 (70), 625–714 (89), 714–833 (119), and 833–1000 (167) are all equivalent intervals. Essentially, this transforms speeds (msec/item) into rates (items/msec).

TABLE 1
Means and Standard Deviations for Word-Recognition Ability Groups

	Superior[a]		High[b]		Avg100[c]		Avg90[d]		Low[e]		Very Low[f]		Total[g]	
	M	SD	M	SD	M	SD	M	SD	M	SD	M	SD	M	SD
Age	30	12.6	24	8.3	22	5.6	26	9.3	28	9.3	34	8.4	27	9.3
Word recognition (WRAT)	122	1.6	114	3.6	104	2.6	94	2.1	84	3.3	72	6.1	97	15.9
Comprehension (WIAT)	110	12.9	110	10.2	93	10.3	94	11.1	85	8.8	74	10.3	93	15.6
Sentence (% correct)	96	3	96	4	88	14	91	11	85	14	68	16	87	15
Decoding (% correct)														
Word naming	99	1	100	1	98	3	97	4	92	7	70	18	93	13
Pseudoword naming	96	5	94	6	92	6	85	11	72	15	48	26	81	21
Single-word decoding	97	2	92	6	89	6	85	8	70	11	59	11	81	15
Paired-word decoding	100	1	98	3	92	7	87	13	74	15	61	13	85	17
Basic speed of processing														
RNN	334	36	326	71	394	102	411	92	431	80	482	120	400	102
PERC–RT[i]	430	85	393	60	436	104	526	235	511	139	597	246	482	172
Digit[h]	449	36	469	68	529	98	533	92	574	107	593	74	531	97
Picture[h]	623	35	619	63	692	115	640	87	741	153	804	269	690	153
DS speed–Decoding[h]														
Word naming	494	41	524	86	672	210	677	205	899	523	1,114	369	742	360
Pseudoword naming	549	72	568	87	737	237	809	216	1,006	499	1,439	764	861	480
DS speed–Decision tasks[i]														
Single-word decoding	895	179	878	170	1,031	215	1,077	174	1,240	375	1,120	445	1,057	306
Paired-word decoding	1,559	230	1,845	696	2,321	831	2,664	985	3,360	1,469	3,791	2,262	2,661	1,431
Sentence task decoding	2,143	446	2,229	469	2,755	528	3,071	933	3,759	699	4,268	980	3,091	1,007

Note. All main effects of group significant; *F*-test values in body text; WRAT = Wide Range Achievement Test; RNN = rapid number naming (msec/item); PERC–RT = perceptual–motor reaction time; DS = domain-specific. WIAT = Weschler Individual Achievement Test.

[a]*n* = 7. [b]*n* = 18. [c]*n* = 20. [d]*n* = 17. [e]*n* = 19. [f]*n* = 14. [g]*n* = 95. [h]*n* = Voice onset times in msec/item. [i]*n* = Reaction times in msec/item.

TABLE 2
Correlation Matrix of Age (Years), Published Tests (Standard Score Units), Accuracy Scores (% Correct), and Rate (items/msec)

	% Correct							Rate[a]								
	WRAT	WIAT	Word	Pseudo-word	Single Word	Paired Word	Sentence	RNN	PERC-RT	Digit	Picture	Word	Pseudo-word	Single Word	Paired Word	Sentence
Accuracy																
WRAT	—															
WIAT	.72	—														
Word naming	.69	.55	—													
Pseudoword	.71	.49	.77	—												
Single-word decoding	.78	.59	.64	.83	—											
Paired-word decoding	.75	.49	.63	.79	.83	—										
Sentence	.51	.48	.51	.53	.55	.51	—									
Rate[a]																
RNN	.39	.34	.36	.35	.43	.49	.40	—								
PERC-RT	.50	.38	.53	.48	.39	.50	.30	.42	—							
Digit	.50	.52	.38	.39	.44	.51	.25	.61	.54	—						
Picture	.38	.38	.37	.32	.39	.46	.19	.52	.46	.78	—					
Word naming	.68	.59	.57	.45	.51	.56	.31	.39	.62	.72	.54	—				
Pseudoword	.69	.61	.51	.51	.58	.57	.34	.41	.56	.70	.54	.82	—			
Single-word decoding	.36	.31	.04	.03	.10	.15	-.06	.07	.36	.40	.31	.54	.52	—		
Paired-word decoding	.52	.40	.17	.22	.32	.28	.17	.30	.40	.52	.34	.60	.62	.64	—	
Sentence	.72	.61	.48	.51	.57	.64	.32	.47	.57	.62	.47	.68	.61	.48	.59	—
Age	-.30	-.19	-.27	-.43	-.43	-.55	-.39	-.42	-.19	.26	-.20	-.25	-.30	-.10	-.22	-.35

Note. The $p < .05$ significance level is $r > .21$. WRAT = Wide Range Achievement Test–Reading (Comprehension); RNN = rapid number naming; PERC–RT = perceptual–motor reaction time. WIAT = Wechsler Individual Achievement Test (Word Recognition Ability); WIAT = Wechsler Individual Achievement

[a]Response times correlations are based on rates (items/msec; i.e., inverse of msec/item).

Passage and sentence comprehension.   A significant main effect of skill group was found on WIAT reading comprehension, $F(3, 70) = 19.45$, $p < .0001$. Post hoc Scheffé tests showed that the high group's performance was significantly different from all other groups. The two high-ability groups (high and superior) each have standard comprehension (WIAT) scores equal to each other but lower than their word-recognition (WRAT) standard scores. The two average-ability groups also have equivalent WIAT scores about 10 points (two thirds SD) below the high-ability groups. The low group was about 10 points lower than the average groups, and the very low group was 10 points below that. In the very low, low, and avg90 groups, word recognition and comprehension means are more closely aligned. This tighter correlation was also evident in a scatterplot of the WIAT–WRAT, showing a weakening of the correlation at the high end of the scale.

The sentence task was marginally significant, $F(3, 70) = 2.66$, $p = .055$, with no significant contrasts among the groups ($p > .05$). Performance on the sentence task showed smaller mean group differences overall, with the only decrease in performance evident for the very low group. Sentence task performance was moderately correlated with comprehension ($r = .49$) and word recognition ($r = .51$) with limits set by ceiling effects.

Decoding tasks.   Significant main effects of skill group were found for decoding task performance measures of word naming, $F(3, 70) = 10.29$, $p < .0001$; pseudoword naming, $F(3, 70) = 18.59$, $p < .0001$; paired-word decoding, $F(3, 70) = 18.52$, $p < .0001$; and single-word decoding, $F(3, 67) = 26.92$, $p < .0001$. Post hoc Scheffé tests showed a significant contrast between the low group and all other groups ($p < .05$) on all four decoding tasks. The high groups performance was also significantly different from the avg90 group in the paired-word task.

The pattern of results in decoding tasks shows near ceiling level performance by the high-ability groups, with declines in performance for each lower ability group. Real-word recognition is near ceiling for the high- and average-ability groups, with only a small decline in the low-ability group (92%) and then a steeper decrease in the very low group (70%). The correlations of the four decoding tasks to word recognition were all strong ($r = .69–.78$).

Basic speed/rate of processing.   Significant main effects of skill group were found for all basic processing speed measures: RNN, $F(3, 70) = 4.94$, $p < .01$; PERC–RT reaction time, $F(3, 70) = 6.35$, $p < .001$; digit naming, $F(3, 70) = 4.77$, $p < .01$; and picture naming, $F(3, 70) = 4.37$, $p < .01$. Post hoc Scheffé tests showed a significant contrast between the high and both the low and avg90 groups ($p < .05$) for RNN and PERC–RT and significant contrast between the high and low groups ($p < .05$) for digit and picture naming.

Domain-specific (decoding and sentence) task speed/rate of processing. Significant main effects of skill group were found for the domain-specific processing speed/rate measures: word naming, $F(3, 70) = 8.95, p < .0001$; pseudoword naming, $F(3, 70) = 12.24, p < .0001$; paired-word decoding, $F(3, 70) = 9.94, p < .0001$; single-word decoding $F(3, 70) = 7.07, p < .001$; and the sentence task, $F(3, 70) = 17.86, p < .0001$. Post hoc Scheffé tests showed a significant contrast between the high group and all other groups ($p < .05$) on the naming tasks (word and pseudoword) and the sentence task. The high group was significantly different from the low and avg90 group on the single- and paired-word decoding tasks. Finally, the avg100 group was significantly different from the low group in the sentence task.

The pattern of responses across all speed/rate measures reflects the group ability differences. The two high-ability groups have approximately the same mean response speeds, with faster speeds than all other groups on all measures. The magnitude of the group differences as measured in speed per item increases from small differences in basic speed measures (digit, picture, PERC–RT, and RNN) to larger differences for all four decoding speed measures and finally the largest difference in the sentence task. Correlations of speed/rate measures to word recognition were high for the sentence task ($r = .72$) and lexical-level naming tasks ($r = .68$ and .69 for word and pseudoword, respectively), and moderate for digit, RNN, and the single-word decoding task ($r = .50, .50,$ and .52, respectively). Finally, small to moderate correlations were found for paired-word decoding, picture naming, and PERC–RT (.36, .38, and .39, respectively).

Skill Group Differences by Task Complexity

To explore the influence of stimulus complexity on speed and accuracy, analyses were run for skill group by task complexity for word naming (syllables), pseudoword naming (letters), and single- versus paired-word decoding.

Word naming. Word naming performance and rate were analyzed with skill group as the between-subjects factor and syllables (one, two, and three) as a within-subject repeated factor. Perhaps poor performance or the slow rates in word naming among the lower ability subgroups is isolated in the longer items. To test this hypothesis, the word items were split into one-, two-, and three-syllable lists. Each list was balanced for frequency of occurrence based on Kucera and Francis (1967). For performance, there was a significant main effect of skill group, $F(3, 70) = 4.57, p < .01$, and syllables, $F(2, 70) = 9.83, p < .0001$, and a significant Skill Group × Syllables interaction, $F(6, 140) = 2.94, p < .01$. One- and two-syllable words were significantly different than three-syllable words in the low group ($p <$

.05). For rate, there was a significant main effect of skill group, $F(2, 70) = 8.95, p < .0001$, and syllables, $F(2, 70) = 34.01, p < .0001$, and a significant Skill Group × Syllables interaction, $F(6, 140) = 3.10, p < .01$. One- and two-syllable words were significantly different than three-syllable words in the low group ($p < .05$).

Pseudoword naming.   Pseudoword naming performance and rate were analyzed with skill group as the between-subjects factor and letters (two, three, four, and five) as a within-subject repeated factor. Perhaps poor performance or slow rates in pseudoword naming among the lower ability subgroups is isolated in the longer items. The four- and five-letter items each include at least one consonant cluster, a feature that may make them both more difficult to decode and pronounce. To test this hypothesis, the words in the list were split into four lists by numbers of letters per item (two to five).[6] In performance, there was a significant main effect of skill group, $F(3, 66) = 18.59, p < .0001$, and letters, $F(3, 66) = 36.82, p < .0001$. The Skill Group × Letters interaction approached, but was not, significant, $F(9, 198) = 1.72, p = .06$. For rate, there was a significant main effect of skill group, $F(3, 66) = 12.24, p < .0001$, and letters, $F(3, 66) = 75.46, p < .0001$, but the Skill Group × Letters interaction was not significant, $F(9, 198) = .60, p = .80$. Post hoc Scheffé tests showed a significant contrast between the high group and all other groups ($p < .05$).

Single- versus paired-word decoding.   No significant interactions were found for accuracy or rate in this analysis. The high group was able to process the paired-word items at about two times the speed of single-word items, whereas the lesser ability groups took more than twice the time in the paired- versus single-word items. However, rates were not significantly different.

Skill Group Score Pattern Comparisons

In this section patterns of results for each of the different ability groups are reported across tasks. Results are described in terms of differences in decoding accuracy, basic speed of processing, speed of processing on decoding tasks, and sentence and passage comprehension. Patterns across variables within the skilled reading high group are discussed first, followed by a discussion contrasting the performance of the low group, with a few comments on the extreme and average groups to round

---

[6]There were 8 items each for the two- and three-letter lists and 16 items each for the four- and five-letter lists.

TABLE 3
Word Naming by Group by Syllable: Accuracy (% Correct) and Speed (msec/Word)

	Superior		High		Avg100		Avg90		Low		Very Low		Total	
	M	SD	M	SD	M	SD	M	SD	M	SD	M	SD	M	SD
Accuracy														
1-SYL	99	4	99	2	100	3	99	2	94	6	73	20	95	12
2-SYL	100	0	100	0	98	6	97	6	94	7	78	21	95	12
3-SYL	99	4	100	0	97	5	96	7	89	16	58	23	90	18
Speed														
1-SYL	495	54	511	86	631	161	634	166	767	292	1,008	357	681	268
2-SYL	495	44	528	81	684	225	676	163	895	592	1,120	373	745	378
3-SYL	491	34	536	79	711	277	726	301	1,118	917	1,317	628	834	575

Note.   All main effects of group significant; F-test values in body of text; SYL = syllable.

out the discussion. Figures 1 through 6 show line graphs of the mean differences among groups. The tasks are grouped so as to facilitate visual interpretations.

High group.   Vellutino, Scanlon, and Sipay (1997) looked at growth curves of young children grouped by overall ability and observed that even after remediation, the highest ability group maintained a considerable advantage over the average-level readers in most measures. They interpreted this finding as an indication that the high-ability readers may have had a near optimal mix of cognitive abilities underlying their reading. The same observation can be made of the high-ability group in this study. The high group was generally fastest, most accurate, and most efficient on all tasks.

Decoding task accuracy for the high group was at ceiling levels on all of the lexical level tasks. As a group, they missed on average less than one item in pseudoword naming,[7] one item in the paired-word task, and three items per 40-item block in the single-word task.

The speed profile of the high-ability group shows their processing efficiency. The average speed on the RNN task was 326 msec/item. This translates to a 200-digit/min oral naming rate. The means across the three blocks were 303, 309, and 318 msec/digit, respectively, well under the 372 (60), 422 (58), and 468 (62) msec/digit norm levels for 14-year-olds. In the digit naming task, the mean was 469 msec/digit—a 143-msec difference from the RNN task. The average PERC–RT speed fell between these two rates at 393 msec/item. By contrast,

---

[7]Three pseudoword items (*plaj, brom,* and *sper*) were the source of over 80% of the errors in the high groups. Over 90% of these errors were consistent alternative vowel sounds (e.g., *broom* for *brom* or *spear* for *sper*). The high group chose one pronunciation alternative and repeated it or self-corrected on second trial.

TABLE 4
Pseudoword Naming by Group by Item Type: Accuracy (% Correct) and Voice Onset Time (msec/Word)

	Superior		High		Avg100		Avg90		Low		Very Low		Total	
	M	SD	M	SD	M	SD	M	SD	M	SD	M	SD	M	SD
Accuracy														
2-letter (CV, VC)	96	6	97	7	96	7	99	3	87	18	69	30	92	17
3-letter (CVC)	95	10	99	4	91	10	88	12	76	24	53	29	85	21
4-letter (CCVC, CCVC)	91	11	82	11	83	13	72	14	63	18	40	21	72	21
5-letter (CCVCC)	97	3	91	9	92	5	80	18	65	17	46	32	79	23
Voice Onset Time														
2-letter (CV, VC)	477	42	510	597	646	195	666	125	873	427	883	340	883	340
3-letter (CVC)	541	80	547	62	704	217	770	173	899	335	1,207	352	1,207	352
4-letter (CCVC, CCVC)	563	77	587	114	781	304	867	254	1,080	613	1,289	490	1,289	490
5-letter (CCVCC)	577	96	595	121	789	254	896	302	1,148	627	1,489	794	1,489	794

Note. All main effects of group significant; *F*-test values in body of text; C = consonant; V = vowel.

TABLE 5
Speed of Response Tasks as a Ratio of Digit Naming Speed

	Superior	High	Avg100	Avg90	Low	Very Low
RNN	0.74	0.70	0.74	0.77	0.75	0.81
PERC–RT	0.96	0.84	0.82	0.99	0.89	1.01
Digits	1.00	1.00	1.00	1.00	1.00	1.00
Pictures	1.39	1.32	1.31	1.20	1.29	1.35
Words	1.10	1.12	1.27	1.27	1.57	1.88
Pseudowords	1.22	1.21	1.39	1.52	1.75	2.42

Note.   RNN = rapid number naming; PERC–RT = perceptual motor reaction time.

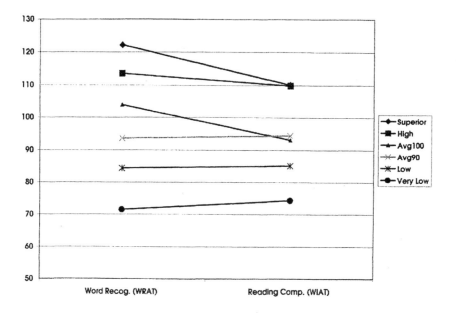

FIGURE 1   Standard scores for ability groups on Word Recognition (WRAT) and Reading Comprehension (WIAT).

the picture naming speed (619 msec/item) was slower by 123 msec/item on average than digit naming. The differences between sequential naming (e.g., digit) and continuous naming tasks (e.g., RNN) have been found to be critical in identifying the rapid naming subtype in dyslexia (Wolf et al., 2000); however, in this broader sample range, the sequential naming tasks (digit, picture, and PERC–RT) captured at least as much variance in word-recognition ability as RNN.

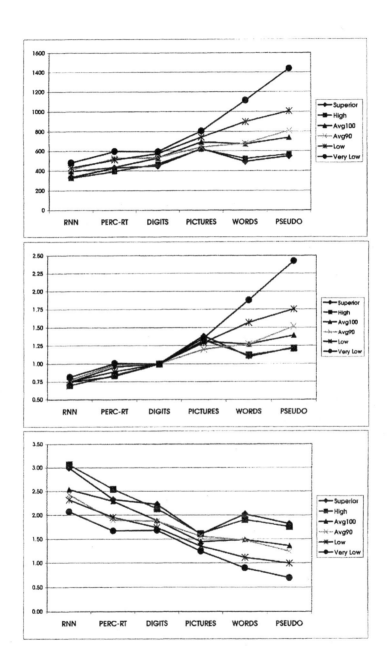

FIGURE 2   Basic speed of processing (RNN, PERC–RT, digits, pictures) and lexical level naming speed tasks (words and pseudowords) by group: Speed (msec/item; top), speed as a ratio of digit naming speed (middle), and rate (items/sec; bottom).

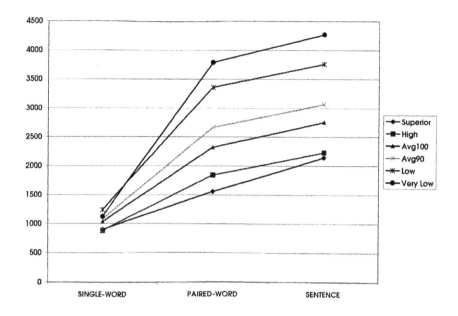

FIGURE 3   Decision tasks (single-, paired-word decoding, and sentence) speeds (msec/item) by group.

Note in Figure 2 the almost linear slope in mean response speeds (60–75 msec) across PERC–RT, digit, word, pseudoword, and picture naming for the high-ability group. Figure 2 (middle) shows the ratios of component skill speeds using digit naming rate means as the divisors. (Ratios calculated by dividing mean response speed of skill group by that group's mean digit naming speed.) There are small persistent advantages for the high group related to the basic processing tasks (RNN, PERC–RT) and a relative disadvantage in picture naming. Word naming shows only about a 10% decrement and pseudoword naming, a 20% decrement relative to digit naming. Both word and pseudoword average naming rates are faster than the time to name line drawings of pictures. This stands in contrast to the lower ability groups. Figure 2 (bottom) shows the same relations transformed into rates (items/sec). In this view, the relative differences among groups as a function of a fixed unit of time is evident, with the high-ability group showing the most efficiency of processing.

The high group's mean reading comprehension score (standard score = 110) is not significantly different in standard score units from their word-recognition scores (standard score = 114). The performance on the sentence task was also high (95% for the group), and mean response rate was slower on average (2,191 msec) than on the lexical-level decoding tasks.

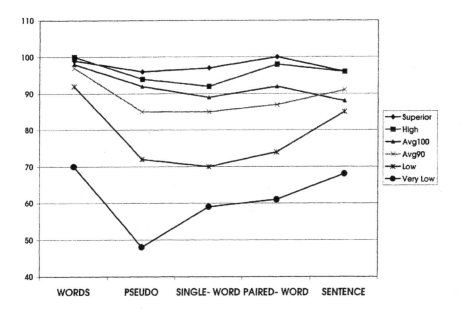

FIGURE 4   Percentage correct on component skill tasks by group.

The superior group ($n = 7$) had the same average reading comprehension levels as the high group, and their component skill profiles were nearly identical. This group included more of the older skilled readers sampled, consequently fixing their WRAT score at the 17- to 19-year-old level may have overestimated their normative word-recognition superiority over the high group. Both groups evidence similar component skill efficiency. The similarity between the two high groups in speed/rate may indicate that they have achieved nearly maximal efficiency in component skills.

Low group.   The pattern of responses of the low group is in strong contrast to the high group's on most tasks. First, decoding task performance was poorer overall and showed variability between the real word versus the three pseudoword decoding tasks. Accuracy at naming real words was relatively high (92%); however, the range of means across the set of pseudoword decoding tasks was between 70% and 75% correct. The maximum scores in the group were 93% on paired-word decoding and 92% on pseudoword naming. The minimum score on pseudoword naming was 45%, that is, even the least able individual could name half of the pseudowords accurately.

Second, the low group evidenced breakdowns in processing speed in the component tasks. Figure 2 shows the disproportionate slowing from PERC–RT speed (top) and digit naming to word and pseudoword naming. The low group may have managed to name 92% of the real words accurately, but they averaged about 900 msec/word, almost ½ sec slower in response time on individual words than the high group. A similar speed gap is evident in naming pseudowords. Recall that (a) the longest pseudoword is five letters in length, (b) all errors are excluded from the mean response computation, and (c) items more than 2 *SD* from the individual's mean are also excluded. The difference is not simply a consequence of slow articulation, because digit and picture naming speeds are faster.

Even in the most basic processing speed tasks there is a significant difference from the high group. RNN averaged 431 msec for the low group. This would translate to an oral reading rate between 133 and 150 words per minute. The low group is approximately 105 to 122 msec slower on average than the high group in digit and picture naming speeds. Although this gap is not as disproportional as the word and pseudoword gap, it is statistically significant and may be practically significant. The average fixation duration for skilled readers in continuous text is about 250 msec/word. Determining what percentage of this speed difference can be attributed to continuous text processing is not possible with this design; however, the potential for processing breakdowns is suggested. Examination of the very low group means shows a continuation of the disproportionate curvilinear relation that was statistically significant for the four central groups, both in speed and accuracy.

When speed is transformed into rate (Figure 2, bottom), the large difference in quantity of information processed per unit time is most apparent. Taken together—the low performance on decoding tasks beginning with the low group and becoming even more pronounced in the very low group—the pattern of evidence is consistent with phonological deficits that may also include very basic level processing speed difficulties, that is, evidence of a double-deficit profile for some members of this group.

The reading comprehension standard scores of the low group are about the same standard score level, on average, as their word-recognition scores, but about 1 *SD* below the mean for 17- to 20-years-olds (sixth to seventh on a grade-level scale). Similarly, sentence task performance is generally poorer in the low group than in the high.

Average ability.   The pattern in the two average-ability groups (avg100, avg90) can be described as highly accurate, but slower, less efficient processing than the high-ability group. Fowler and Scarborough (1993) characterized this profile as nonautomatic readers. The high-ability group was significantly faster than the average groups on all lexical- and sentence-level speed/rate tasks. Both average groups showed similar accuracy scores, but there was a nonsignificant trend toward slower performance in the avg90 relative to the avg100 group. This helps explain why the word naming speed measure was a significant, unique predictor (about

14%) of overall word-recognition ability in multiple regression analyses across the sample, even after accounting for decoding skill variance (Sabatini, in press). Even small differences in speed/rate were correlated with overall word-recognition ability levels.

DISCUSSION

The results of this study can be summarized as follows. With respect to the first research question, there were significant group differences among ability groups on processing task measures. As expected, significant group differences were found for passage comprehension, sentence processing, and decoding accuracy. Significant group differences were also found for basic cognitive, decoding, and sentence rates, that is, on all the processing speed tasks measured. Relative to basic speed measures, the group differences in the word-recognition tasks (real and pseudoword) become disproportionately slower in speed per item as ability decreased. This word-level effect was accompanied by significantly higher error rates specifically attributable to the low-ability group. In addressing the second question, however, stimulus complexity by processing rate interactions across groups were generally not significant. For the one model in which there was a significant interaction, that is, naming rates for three-syllable real words, the result was confounded with higher error rates for three-syllable words in the low group. This outcome is examined in more detail in the following discussion.

With respect to the third question, based on examination of the patterns of results across tasks within groups, we characterized the high group as possessing rapid, efficient word-recognition skills; the average group as possessing accurate, but nonautomatic processing skills; and the low group as struggling with both accuracy and efficiency in basic word-recognition and decoding skills.

We focus discussion first on the speed, rate, and complexity results. Small differences in general processing speed have been found to have direct effects on domain-specific skill performance, as well as on higher order, nontimed cognitive tasks (Fry & Hale, 2000; Kail & Salthouse, 1994). Performance could have become degraded in two ways: (a) Individuals could make more errors, or (b) their response speeds could slow disproportionately as they attempted to manage their resources in performing complex tasks. We had hypothesized that processing speed differences would have significant effects as complexity of task, text, and pattern increased (Just & Carpenter, 1992), not just performance accuracy.

The analyses that were designed to show the effects of complexity on processing, however, were equivocal. The prediction that complexity would have a disproportionate influence on low-ability groups was not strongly upheld. Although complexity showed within-group main effects and had an incremental, nonlinear pattern that was more pronounced in the lower ability groups when speed (msec/item) was plotted, the analyses failed to show significant group by stimulus interactions when rate (items/msec) of processing was measured.

For example, there was a small, incremental increase for each additional letter (two to five) in the pseudoword naming task for a total of 80 msec (see Figure 5), but the effect was attributable to the low-ability group, which also showed performance difficulties as letters were added to the task items. Similar results were found when the word naming task was subdivided by syllable. The superior, high and average groups all scored better than 95% accuracy on all the items (Figure 6, bottom). Performance began to drop to 94% on one- and two-syllable words and to 89% on three-syllable words for the low group. Significant decrements in performance and speed were only obtained for the low group; consequently, speed and accuracy as different factors were confounded.

The inverse transformation of the data from speed (msec/item) to rate (items/msec), which created linear relations across groups, may have been a contributing factor to the lack of statistical significance. Nonetheless, it remains unproven whether or how stimulus and task complexity interacts with speed of processing to influence word-recognition skills.

Despite the lack of significance of the complexity analyses, the cross-task efficiency profiles across groups are still suggestive of a more complex pattern. For example, there were differences both in the average speed (msec/item) and the slopes of the lines in the word naming speeds by syllable (Figure 6, top) and pseudoword naming speeds by letter (Figure 5, top) across groups. The superior and high groups were about 100 msec on average faster than the two average groups on one- and two-syllable words and about 200 msec faster on three-syllable words. The low group, which only showed an average of 5% to 10% drop in performance, showed a 250 msec difference between the high groups on the one-syllable words, which grew to almost 500 msec in the three-syllable words. Finally, the very low ability group showed an even greater disparity in naming speed, as would be expected given their low performance on all items. A similar speed pattern is evident in pseudoword naming, except performance levels drop more precipitously across groups and item types as well.

With respect to single- versus paired-word decoding tasks, the average speed was approximately double for the paired-word (1,603 msec/item) versus single-word (868 msec/item) task items for the high group. The average and low groups, on the other hand, spent more than twice the time per item in the paired-word versus the single-word task. In the paired-word task, there was more information per item to evaluate, but also more information to resolve ambiguity. This likely explains why performance was slightly more efficient (i.e., accurate and faster overall) in the paired-word task for the high group. The most skilled individuals were better able to integrate and coordinate the multiple sources of information to their advantage, without a significant sacrifice of time or efficiency,

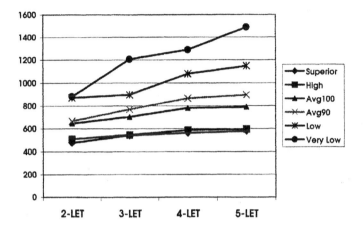

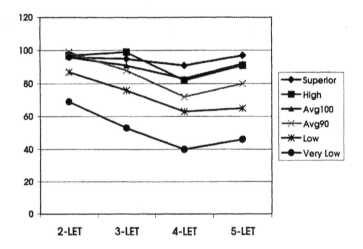

FIGURE 5   Pseudoword naming speeds (msec/item; top) and percentage correct (bottom)
by item type by group.

when compared to the less able individuals. The difference in rate (items/msec),
however, did not significantly interact with group.

Another explanation of the cross-group differences in efficiency is worth considering. Perhaps it is not complexity of stimulus per se but rather the interaction of
speed with the more general, long-term learning task of acquiring robust word-recognition skills that is evident in these patterns. Indirect effects of speed on skill acquisition may accumulate in several ways. Limited working memory resources
(not working memory span per se) could reduce the benefit of experiential learning
that is usually associated with practice in a complex domain. That is, the constant

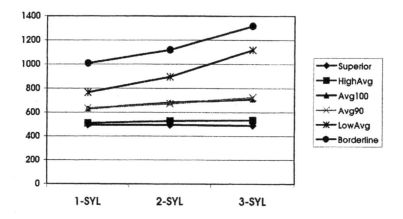

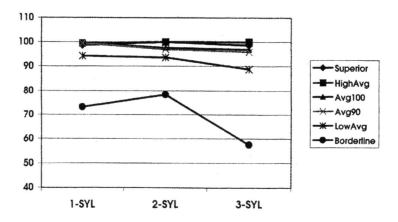

FIGURE 6   Word naming speeds (msec/item; top) and percentage correct (bottom) by syllables by group.

struggle to store and operate on elements in working memory could have the side effect of reducing the gains in long-term knowledge acquisition and proceduralization of skills (Anderson, 1993). Managing more limited resources likely restricts metacognitive processes such as self-monitoring (Reynolds, 2000). These restrictions create a vicious cycle, even when performance is accurate. That is, the slow, laborious effort to decode or recognize a word reduces learning from successful trials. Reduced learning efficiency then leads to reduced component skill automaticity and efficiency, which, in turn, limits the quantity and quality of subsequent learning opportunities and efficiency at all levels of the reading process (e.g., sublexical, lexical, propositional, etc.). Small differences at the event level become cumulative, with quality and quantity of practice and learning determining the rate of long-term growth in the domain. The sum of these possibilities suggests a different take on the Matthew effect (Stanovich, 1986) with a locus internal to the cognitive system, rather than external to motivation and limited environmental experiences. Small, yet significant differences in processing speeds have cumulatively larger influence on long-term learning rates.

The implications of processing speed for acquiring efficient, robust word-recognition ability may be especially important to low- or intermediate-ability adults. School-aged children and adolescents are constantly challenged by the school curriculum, teachers, and parents to read a large volume and variety of texts on a daily basis for several years. Furthermore, there are external incentives to increase efficiency of reading speed to keep up with the demands of the volume of reading. This is no guarantee of successful reading achievement; however, it may provide sufficient opportunity for experience and exposure to texts that, when combined with a quality intervention, may make up for any differences in learning curves related to processing speed. Adults, on the other hand, neither have the same external demands requiring exposure to texts, nor have incentives to make efficiency gains through pushing themselves to process text more rapidly. Given the laboriously slow reading rates also observed in this study, it may be that some modern-day version of speed reading training that does not violate what we know about perceptual span and the reading process (Rayner, 1997) may be necessary to help adults gain in efficiency.

If there aren't any inherent processing limitations or phonological deficits in many adults with low-literacy levels, then training or practice that helps them improve the speed, efficiency, and automaticity of component skills could also have a long-term effect on the acquisition of advanced word-recognition skills. For example, Frederiksen, Warren, and Rosebery (1985) had poor readers practice scanning words for high-frequency letter patterns. The patterns could appear anywhere in the words, a feature used to help the participants learn to spread their attention more evenly across the entire word. The task required not only accurate, but also speeded performance. The authors found not only that speed improved for identifying the target patterns in novel words (i.e., words that were not part of the initial practice set), but also baseline speeds improved for target patterns not yet practiced. That is, the skill of speeded perceptual processing appeared to transfer to other graphemic patterns, independent of item-specific experience. Furthermore, they also found improved performance in untimed nonword decoding. Das-Smaal, Klapwijk, and van der Leij (1996) replicated the study with a larger sample of poor reading Dutch 9- and 10-year-olds, using a control group design, and obtained similar results. Finally, Wolf and Katzir-Cohen (2001) designed and tested an intervention called RAVE-O program (Retrieval, Automaticity, Vocabulary, Engagement, and Orthography) that employs speeded practice on a sample of severely disabled second- and third-grade children. They reported positive results based on preliminary analyses of intervention data (see also Breznitz, 1997; Tressoldi, Lonciari, & Vio, 2000).

Based on the patterns of component skill differences across groups, we hypothesize that small differences in basic speed of processing may interact with long-term learning of word-recognition skills. The data on low-literate adults presented is consistent with this position, although alternate hypothesis are also feasible. Predictions based on this hypothesis can be tested in future research. For example, speed/rate of processing can be used as a predictor of the quantity of decoding training and practice needed to reach thresholds of accuracy or speed of performance. Alternately, basic speed/rate of processing may predict lower word-recognition speed and reading rate plateaus, even after extensive practice and high accuracy are achieved.

To close the discussion, we make note of several limitations the reader should consider. First, the relations found in this study need to be replicated on other samples of adult learners before broad generalizations are warranted. The means, correlations, and general response patterns to the tasks were largely consistent with the vast body of research on component reading skills. However, because there are still only a few studies that have compared samples of low-literate adults with other known groups, caution is warranted.

We acknowledge that having no independent corroboration that participants were in the normal IQ range is a threat to the interpretation of the results for some. Also, specific disability measures, such as testing for attention deficient hyperactivity disorder, would have been helpful in interpreting speed measures in terms of attention disorders, a relation identified as a potential mediating factor/construct in recent studies. In the future, such measures should be included whenever possible. Also, the sample in this study was not balanced for gender differences; there were more men represented in the low-ability groups and more women in the high-ability groups.

Finally, like any correlational study, claims or conclusions concerning causal relations should not be assumed until longitudinal, experimental, and training studies have been conducted. The implications of these findings for understanding different patterns are presented to encourage thinking and discussion about the interaction of speed and accuracy in reading acquisition. In some cases, we have speculated about group differences as if they represent points on different developmental trajectories (as in the differences between high- and average-ability groups). At other times we discussed differences in terms of groups with qualitatively different underlying deficits that might influence those trajectories (as in between the very low versus other groups). We cannot yet draw any firm conclusions about whether speed of processing is cause or consequence in adult reading acquisition, although we think the evidence suggests further study is warranted.

SUMMARY

To summarize, we have presented data on how speed/rate of processing relates to the word-recognition ability of adults. Across the continuum of adult abilities, general speed of processing, as well as word-specific speed of processing, were correlated with overall word-recognition ability. Analyses of subgroups of adults at different levels of word-recognition ability showed significant and pervasive speed/rate differences, as well as differences in accuracy of performance. RAN deficits may be a more specialized case of general processing speed deficits, which manifests a qualitatively different processing subtype. The results here underscore the importance of understanding and establishing theoretical models relating phonological processing and speed of processing to the acquisition of decoding skill and fluency in impaired adult readers.

ACKNOWLEDGMENTS

This research was conducted with the support of the National Center on Adult Literacy through a grant from the Office of Educational Research and Improvement, U.S. Department of Education, and with fellowship support at the University of Delaware. Some of the results here first appeared in my dissertation research (Sabatini, 1997), and other analyes of this data are also to appear in Sabatini (2002).

Thanks to Richard L. Venezky, and staff and students at Educational Technology Laboratory at the University of Delaware, as well as the adult educators and students who participated in the study.

REFERENCES

Abadzi, H. (1996). Does age diminish the ability to learn fluent reading? *Educational Psychology Review, 8,* 373–396.

Anderson, J. R. (1993). *Rules of the mind.* Hillsdale, NJ: Lawrence Erlbaum Associates, Inc.

Bell, L. C., & Perfetti, C. A. (1994). Reading Skill: Some adult comparisons. *Journal of Educational Psychology, 86,* 244–255.

Bernell Corporation. (n.d.). *New York State Optometric Association King-Devick Test Cards.* South Bend, IN: Author.

Booth, J. R., Perfetti, C. A., MacWhinney, B., & Hunt, S. B. (2000). The association of rapid temporal perception with orthographic and phonological processing in children and adults with reading impairment. *Scientific Studies of Reading, 4,* 77–100.

Bowers, P. G., Sunseth, K., & Golden, J. (1999). The route between rapid naming and reading progress. *Scientific Studies of Reading, 3,* 31–53.

Bowers, P. G., & Wolf, M. (1993). Theoretical links among naming speed, precise timing mechanisms and orthographic skill in dyslexia. *Reading and Writing: An Interdisciplinary Journal, 5*(1), 69–85.

Breznitz, Z. (1997). Enhancing the reading of dyslexic children by reading acceleration and auditory masking. *Journal of Educational Psychology, 89,* 103–113.

Bruck, M. (1990). Word-recognition skills of adults with childhood diagnoses of dyslexia. *Developmental Psychology, 26,* 439–454.

Byrne, B., & Ledez, J. (1983). Phonological awareness in reading-disabled adults. *Australian Journal of Psychology, 35,* 185–197.

Carver, R. P. (1997). Reading for one second, one minute, or one year from the perspective of Rauding Theory. *Scientific Studies of Reading, 1,* 3–43.

Carver, R. P., & David, A. H. (2001). Investigating reading achievement using a causal model. *Scientific Studies of Reading, 5,* 107–140.

Clark, H. H., & Chase, W. G. (1972). On the process of comparing sentences against pictures. *Cognitive Psychology, 3,* 472–517.

Das-Smaal, E. A., Klapwijk, M. J. G., & van der Leij, A. (1996). Training of perceptual unit processing in children with a reading disability. *Cognition and Instruction, 14,* 221–250.

Denckla, M. B., & Rudel, R. G. (1976). Rapid "automatized" naming (R.A.N.): Dyslexia differentiation from other learning disabilities. *Neuropsychologia, 14,* 471–479.

Farmer, M. E., & Klein, R. M. (1995). The evidence for a temporal processing deficit linked to dyslexia: A review. *Psychonomic Bulletin & Review, 2,* 460–493.

Fink, R. P. (1998). Literacy development in successful men and women with dyslexia. *Annals of Dyslexia, 68,* 311–346.

Fowler, A. E., & Scarborough, H. S. (1993). *Should reading-disabled adults be distinguished from other adults seeking literacy instruction? A review of theory and research* (Tech. Rep. No. TR93–7). University of Pennsylvania, National Center on Adult Literacy.

Frederiksen, J. R., Warren, B. M., & Rosebery, A. S. (1985). A componential approach to training reading skills: Pt. 1. Perceptual units training. *Cognition and Instruction, 2,* 91–130.

Fry, A. F., & Hale, S. (1996). Processing speed, working memory, and fluid intelligence: Evidence for a developmental cascade. *Psychological Science, 7,* 237–241.

Fry, A. F., & Hale, S. (2000). Relationships among processing speed, working memory, and fluid intelligence in children. *Biological Psychology, 54,* 1–34.

Gathercole, S. E., & Baddeley, A. D. (1993). *Working memory and language.* Hillsdale, NJ: Lawrence Erlbaum Associates, Inc.

Greenberg, D., Ehri, L. C., & Perin, D. (1997). Are word-reading processes the same or different in adult literacy students and third–fifth graders matched for reading level? *Journal of Educational Psychology, 89,* 262–275.

Jastak & Associates. (1993). *Wide Range Achievement Test.* Wilmington, DE: Author.

Just, M. A., & Carpenter, P. A. (1992). A capacity theory of comprehension: Individual differences in working memory. *Psychological Review, 99*(1), 122–149.

Kail, R., & Hall, L. (1994). Processing speed, naming speed, and reading. *Developmental Psychology, 30,* 949–954.

Kail, R., Hall, L. K., & Caskey, B. J. (1999). Processing speed, exposure to print, and naming speed. *Applied Psycholinguistics, 20,* 303–314.

Kail, R., & Park, Y.-S. (1994). Processing time, articulation time, and memory span. *Journal of Experimental Child Psychology, 57,* 281–291.

Kail, R., & Salthouse, T. A. (1994). Processing speed as a mental capacity. *Acta Psychologica, 86,* 199–225.

Klein, R. M., & Farmer, M. E. (1995). Dyslexia and temporal processing deficit: A review of the literature. *Psychological Bulletin and Review, 2,* 460–493.

Kucera, H., & Francis, W. N. (1967). *Computational analysis of present-day American English.* Providence, RI: Brown University Press.

Manis, F. R., Seidenberg, M. S., & Doi, L. M. (1999). See Dick RAN: Rapid naming and the longitudinal prediction of reading subskills in first and second graders. *Scientific Studies of Reading, 3,* 129–157.

National Reading Panel. (2000). *Teaching children to read: An evidence-based assessment of the scientific research literature on reading and its implications for reading instruction.* Washington, DC: National Institute of Child Health and Human Development.

Pennington, B. F., Van Orden, G. C., Smith, S. D., Green, P. A., & Haith, M. M. (1990). Phonological processing skills and deficits in adult dyslexics. *Child Development, 61,* 1753–1778.

Perfetti, C. A. (1985). *Reading ability.* New York: Oxford University Press.

Pratt, A. C., & Brady, S. (1988). Relation of phonological awareness to reading disability. *Journal of Educational Psychology, 80,* 319–323.

Psychological Corporation. (1990). *Wechsler Individual Achievement Tests: Reading Comprehension.* San Antonio, TX: Author.

Rayner, K. (1997). Understanding eye movements in reading. *Scientific Studies of Reading, 1,* 317–339.

Rayner, K., Pollatsek, A., & Bilsky, A. B. (1995). Can a temporal processing deficit account for dyslexia? *Psychonomic Bulletin & Review, 2,* 501–507.

Read, C., & Ruyter, L. (1985). Reading and spelling skills in adults of low literacy. *Remedial and Special Education, 6*(6), 43–52.

Reynolds, R. E. (2000). Attentional resource emancipation: Toward understanding the interaction of word identification and comprehension processes in reading. *Scientific Studies of Reading, 4,* 169–196.

Ross-Gordon, J. M. (1998). Literacy education for adults with learning disabilities: Perspectives from the adult education side of the mirror. In S. A. Vogel & S. Reder (Eds.), *Learning disabilities, literacy, and adult education* (pp. 69–88). Baltimore: Brookes.

Sabatini, J. P. (1997). *Is accuracy enough? The cognitive implications of speed of response in adult reading ability.* Unpublished doctoral dissertation, University of Delaware, Newark.

Sabatini, J. P. (2002). Word reading processes in adult learners. In E. Assink & D. Sandra (Eds.), *Reading complex words: Cross-language studies.* London: Kluwer Academic.

Sabatini, J. P., Venezky, R. L., Jain, R., & Kharik, P. (2000). *Cognitive reading assessments for low literate adults: An analytic review and new framework* (TR00–01). University of Pennsylvania, National Center on Adult Literacy.

Salthouse, T. A. (1991). *Theoretical perspectives on cognitive aging.* Hillsdale, NJ: Lawrence Erlbaum Associates, Inc.

Salthouse, T. A. (1992). *Mechanisms of age-cognition relations in adulthood.* Hillsdale, NJ: Lawrence Erlbaum Associates, Inc.

Share, D. L., & Stanovich, K. E. (1995). Cognitive processes in early reading development: Accommodating individual differences into a model of acquisition. *Issues in Education, 1,* 1–57.

Stanovich, K. E. (1986). Matthew effects in reading: Some consequences of individual differences in the acquisition of literacy. *Reading Research Quarterly, 21,* 360–406.

Stringer, R., & Stanovich, K. E. (2000). The connection between reaction time and variation in reading ability: Unravelling covariance relationships with cognitive ability and phonological sensitivity. *Scientific Studies of Reading, 4,* 41–53.

Studdert-Kennedy, M., & Mody, M. (1995). Auditory temporal perception deficits in the reading-impaired: A critical review of the evidence. *Psychonomic Bulletin and Review, 2,* 508–514.

Tabachnick, B. G., & Fidell, L. S. (1989). *Using multivariate statistics* (2nd ed.). New York: HarperCollins.

Tallal, P., Miller, S. L., Jenkins, W. M., & Merzenich, M. M. (1997). The role of temporal processing in developmental language-based learning disorders: An underlying difficulty of poor readers. In B. Blachman (Ed.), *Foundations of reading acquisition and dyslexia: Implications for early intervention* (pp. 49–66). Mahwah, NJ: Lawrence Erlbaum Associates, Inc.

Torgesen, J. K. (1997). Contributions of phonological awareness and rapid automatic naming ability to the growth of word-reading skills in second- to fifth-grade children. *Scientific Studies of Reading, 1,* 161–185.

Tressoldi, P. E., Lonciari, I., & Vio, C. (2000). Treatment of specific developmental reading disorders, derived from single-and dual-route models. *Journal of Learning Disabilities, 33,* 278–285.

Vellutino, F. R., Scanlon, D. M., & Sipay, E. R. (1997). Toward distinguishing between congitive and experiential deficits as primary sources of difficulty in learning to read: The importance of early intervention in diagnosing specific reading disability. In B. Blachman (Ed.), *Foundations of reading acquisition and dyslexia: Implications for early intervention* (pp. 347–380). Mahwah, NJ: Lawrence Erlbaum Associates, Inc.

Wimmer, H., Mayringer, H., & Landerl, K. (1998). Poor reading: A deficit in skill-automatization or a phonological deficit? *Scientific Studies of Reading, 2,* 321–340.

Wolf, M. (1991). Naming speed and reading: The contribution of the cognitive neurosciences. *Reading Research Quarterly, 26,* 123–141.

Wolf, M. (1997). A provisional, integrative account of phonological and naming-speed deficits in dyslexia: Implications for diagnosis and intervention. In B. Blachman (Ed.), *Foundations of reading acquisition and dyslexia: Implications for early intervention* (pp. 67–92). Mahwah, NJ: Lawrence Erlbaum Associates, Inc.

Wolf, M., & Bowers, P. (1999). The "double deficit hypothesis" for the developomental dyslexias. *Journal of Educational Psychology, 91,* 1–24.

Wolf, M., & Bowers, P. G. (2000). Naming-speed deficits in developmental reading disabilities: An introduction to the special issue on the double-deficit hypothesis. *Journal of Learning Disabilities, 33,* 322–324.

Wolf, M., Bowers, P. G., & Biddle, K. (2000). Naming-speed processes, timing, and reading: A conceptual review. *Journal of Learning Disabilities, 33,* 387–407.

Wolf, M., & Katzir-Cohen, T. (2001). Reading fluency and its intervention. *Scientific Studies of Reading, 5,* 211–239.

Manuscript received June 14, 2001
Final revision received November 28, 2001
Accepted December 1, 2001

SCIENTIFIC STUDIES OF READING, 6(3), 299–316
Copyright © 2002, Lawrence Erlbaum Associates, Inc.

Patterns of Word-Recognition Errors Among Adult Basic Education Native and Nonnative Speakers of English

Rosalind Kasle Davidson and John Strucker

National Center for the Study of Adult Learning and Literacy
Harvard University Graduate School of Education

Numerous studies have documented the decoding difficulties of adult basic education (ABE) students in the United States. However, the native speakers of English (NSE) and nonnative speakers of English (NNSE) in ABE classes present different reading behaviors. To explore this, 90 low–intermediate readers (45 NSE and 45 NNSE) were matched on pseudoword reading (Woodcock Reading Mastery Test–Revised; Woodcock, 1987). Their substitution errors in word recognition (Diagnostic Assessments of Reading; Roswell & Chall, 1992) were then classified as phonetically plausible, phonetically implausible, or real words. Both groups made similar numbers of phonetically implausible errors. However, although both possessed comparable pseudoword decoding skills, NSE made more real-word substitutions than NNSE, and NNSE made more phonetically plausible substitutions than NSE. This suggests that ABE teachers should not only be aware of how much decoding students know but also to what extent they actually use that knowledge when reading.

A number of studies have documented the word-recognition and word analysis difficulties among adult basic education (ABE) and adult secondary education (ASE) students in the United States (Greenberg, Ehri, & Perin, 1997, 2002/this issue; Sabatini, 2002/this issue; Shafir & Siegel, 1994; Snow & Strucker, 2000; Strucker, 1995, 1997). For example, Read and Ruyter (1985), Read (1988a, 1988b), and Pratt and Brady (1988) reported that the reading of adult literacy students who read below grade equivalent (GE) 6 tended to resemble the reading of reading disabled

Requests for reprints should be sent to Rosalind K. Davidson, National Center for the Study of Adult Learning and Literacy, 303 Nichols House, Appian Way, Harvard University Graduate School of Education, Cambridge, MA 02138.

Grade 3 to 6 children rather than that of normally progressing younger readers. Johnson and Blalock (1987), Spreen and Haaf (1986), and Bruck (1990, 1992) found persistent word-recognition deficits even among adults with dyslexia who had achieved college levels of silent reading comprehension, and Fink (1998) found the same pattern among highly successful adults who had been identified as having dyslexia in childhood.

This article is based on data from the National Center for the Study of Adult Learning and Literacy Adult Reading Components Study (ARCS; Strucker & Davidson, 2002). The ARCS assessed and interviewed 676 ABE/ASE learners enrolled at adult literacy centers whose reading ranged from beginning through high school levels and above. We focus here on 212 of the 676 learners who scored between GE 4 and GE 6 in word recognition. Adult literacy teachers are usually well aware that learners below GE 4 need instruction in word analysis and word recognition. However, they often do not realize that many adults above GE 4 may also need to improve their decoding and fluency if they are to make smooth progress toward higher levels of reading.

In the Harvard Adult Reading Lab we have found that adults at the GE 4 to 6 level make markedly slower progress than those who come to us with slightly higher GE 7 to 8 decoding abilities. One reason for this may be a greater prevalence of reading disability among the GE 4 to 6 learners. The ARCS interview data suggest that the childhood reading difficulties among GE 4 to 6 learners had been noticed by their K–12 teachers. Sixty-five percent of the GE 4 to 6 U.S.-born learners reported receiving extra help in reading in childhood, including Chapter 1, special education placement, and other forms of tutoring as compared with 45% for those at GE 7 to 8 and 35% for those at GE 9 to 12 (Strucker & Davidson, 2002).

Whereas the studies of adult learners cited have analyzed the word recognition, phonemic awareness, and in some instances the spelling abilities of adult literacy students, these studies have focused exclusively on the reading of native speakers of English (NSE). However, in many parts of the United States, substantial numbers of nonnative speakers of English (NNSE) are enrolled in ABE classes rather than classes designed specifically as English for Speakers of Other Languages (ESOL). For example, among the total ARCS ABE learners, 42% reported that they were not native speakers of English; of the 212 learners at GE 4 to 6, 25.5% reported that they were not NSE (Strucker & Davidson, 2002).

The reading behavior of NSE and NNSE, even when matched for level, may not be identical. NSE and NNSE present different component reading patterns or profiles, based on clinical observation and reports (Chall, 1994; Strucker, 1995, 1997). Chall described the differences between the nonnative and the native speakers in the Harvard Adult Reading Lab as follows:

> We began to be aware of two patterns of scores—one that was common among adults
> for whom English was a second language; the other resembled the patterns of

strengths and weaknesses found among children and adolescents who tend to be diagnosed as having learning disabilities.

We found the non-native speaking group ... to be relatively stronger in the ... [word] recognition or print aspects of reading, as distinguished from the meaning or comprehension aspects.

The "learning disability" pattern ... [includes] ... adults ... who are relatively stronger in word meaning and relatively weaker in the print aspects of reading—word recognition and analysis, spelling and oral reading. (p. 30)

Possible differences between NSE and NNSE led us to our first three research questions.

1. Would the pattern of relatively stronger print versus meaning skills in NNSE emerge in the GE 4 to 6 data?
2. Would the pattern of relatively stronger meaning versus print skills in NSE emerge in the GE 4 to 6 data?
3. When matched for word recognition and pseudoword decoding, would the patterns of word-recognition errors made by NSE differ from those made by NNSE in the GE 4 to 6 data?

The 77 nonnative speakers in the GE 4 to 6 range come from diverse linguistic and educational backgrounds, especially with regard to their exposure to spoken English and formal schooling in English. Some came to the United States as adults and acquired English primarily from ESOL classes, whereas others came to the United States as young children and acquired all or substantial amounts of their childhood schooling in English. Our fourth research question explores this area of exposure to English.

4. Do the patterns of word-recognition errors of nonnative speakers differ depending on whether their exposure to English took place before or after age 12?

METHOD

Participants

ARCS participants were randomly selected by lottery within each class, at each of the 30 literacy centers participating in the study. The number of participants from each class was proportionate to its enrollment. The ARCS battery for ABE/ASE learners took between 1.5 and 2.5 hr to complete, and learners were paid $10 per hour or part of an hour for their time.

To take differences among the nonnative speakers' length of exposure to English into account, we divided them into two groups: those who reported learning English before the age of 12 (NNSE < 12) and those who learned it from age 12 or older (NNSE > 12). Although the age 12 division is somewhat arbitrary, it does attempt to reflect differences between those exposed to environmental oral English and to reading instruction in English before secondary education and those exposed at a later age. For error analyses of the GE 4 to 6 group, three subgroups (NNE, NNSE < 12, NNSE > 12) with equivalent distributions of word attack raw scores were formed by selecting a range of participants around the full group mean on the Woodcock Reading Mastery Test–Revised (WRMT–R; Woodcock, 1987) Word Attack frequency list.

Instruments

The ARCS battery included a 66-item questionnaire and 17 separate reading assessments.[1] The comparisons in this study are based on the following measures.

Diagnostic Assessments of Reading (DAR; Roswell & Chall, 1992).
The DAR is an individually administered reading achievement battery that yields GE scores from GE 1 to 12 in word recognition, oral reading, silent reading comprehension, word meaning, and spelling. Each DAR subtest is administered through the appropriate grade levels until the student is no longer able to meet the criterion for a given grade level. The DAR combines grade equivalent levels 9 and 10 (GE 9/10) and 11 and 12 (GE 11/12).

DAR Word Recognition.
This subtest of the DAR comprises graded word lists from GE 1 through GE 11/12, with mastery on a level determined by the highest level on which the learner reads 7 out of 10 or more words correctly. DAR Word Recognition was audio recorded.

---

[1]The full ARCS test battery is as follows: Word Analysis (consonant sounds only), Word Recognition, Oral Reading (including rate in syllables per sec), Spelling, Silent Reading Comprehension, Word Meaning (receptive vocabulary) of the Diagnostic Assessments of Reading (Roswell & Chall, 1992); Peabody Picture Vocabulary Test III (Dunn, Dunn, & Dunn, 1997); Word Analysis subtest of the WRMT–R (Woodcock, 1987); Rapid Automatized Naming (colors, letters, numbers, objects, letters and numbers, and colors, letters, and numbers; Wolf, 1991); Test of Auditory Analysis Skills (Rosner, 1975); and the Digit Span and Information subtests of the WAIS–IIIR (Wechsler, 1997).

DAR Silent Reading Comprehension.   This subtest of the DAR consists of graded passages ranging from GE 3 through GE 11/12. The learner is given a total of 5 min to read each short passage and to answer four multiple-choice questions, with three out of four questions correct being the criterion for mastery of a passage.

Word Attack.   The Word Attack subtest from the WRMT–R consists of 45 pseudowords arranged in sets of increasing difficulty from consonant-vowel-consonant words to polysyllabic strings. It was administered according to the examiner's manual directions. In this article we used raw scores rather than standard scores so that we could focus on absolute decoding performances, irrespective of chronological age. WRMT–R Word Attack was recorded.

Peabody Picture Vocabulary Test–III (PPVT–III; Dunn, Dunn, & Dunn, 1997).   The PPVT–III assesses receptive or listening vocabulary. After a target word is pronounced by the examiner, the participant selects one of the four pictures on an easel that best "tells about" the target word. Seventeen sets of 10 words are ordered in increasing difficulty. Administration followed the directions in the examiner's manual with the exception that, to speed administration and as an accommodation to the ABE/ASE population, examiners were trained to begin with sets that were somewhat lower than those corresponding to the learners' chronological ages.

ARCS Background Questionnaire.   The 66-item questionnaire was administered orally. We obtained information on participants' linguistic and educational background, parents' literacy and linguistic background, participants' employment, health, perceived reading difficulties (if any), reading remediation (if any), current literacy practices, and educational goals.

Procedure

Participants were interviewed and tested individually at their learning centers by graduate students or local ABE/ESOL practitioners trained by the investigators (Strucker, Davidson, & Reddy, 1998). To ensure learners' privacy, practitioner interviewers did not test learners at literacy centers where they also taught. Because the questionnaire and some of the tests required on-the-spot judgments by the interviewers, those tests and the questionnaire were recorded on Sony HF–90 audio tape using Sony TCM–59V cassette recorders with internal microphones. Each interview tape was then checked for scoring accuracy by teams of trained graduate students whose interrater reliability was computed and monitored for each assessment.

Error Analysis

Error analysis was conducted on the last and highest level GE of the DAR Word Recognition lists that each participant read—by definition, a list on which fewer than seven words had been pronounced correctly. For each participant it was the most difficult list, the one on which they had the most errors. This final word list determined the highest GE mastery level as being one GE level below. Therefore, the highest GE level word lists that GE 4 to 6 participants read were levels 5, 6, or 7. We considered analyzing performance on all the word lists a participant had read, but the range of grade levels among the group would have complicated comparisons with issues of word frequency and word length.

Listening to tape recordings, two researchers working independently classified each of the 10 words read on the highest list for each participant into one of four categories: correct, phonetically plausible substitutions, not phonetically plausible substitutions, and substitutions of real English words. If the first two scorers disagreed on how to classify a word, a third researcher was brought in for discussion to resolve the issue. Words that were not attempted by participants were not counted in this analysis. Coding criteria for the analysis of word-recognition errors follows.

Correct.   Criteria for correct responses were the same as used in the ARCS (Strucker, Davidson, & Reddy, 1998). All elements corresponding to dictionary pronunciations had to be present, including correct stress and phoneme productions. Native speakers' regional pronunciation differences (e.g., a Texan saying "particuhlar" or "partickler" or a New Englander saying "pahticuluh" for *particular*) were counted as correct. Nonnative speakers' pronunciation features were also counted as correct in the following areas: slight deviations from the difficult English /th/ and /r/ sounds and slight deviations from English short vowel sounds.

Phonetically plausible substitutions.   All phonemes and syllables had to be pronounced in a way that was plausible according to English phonics. Errors could have occurred on stress (e.g., *solitary*; *monotony*) or consist of plausible vowel-sound substitutions (e.g., *man-aige* for *manage*). Wherever there were stress errors, vowels in the resulting syllables had to conform to the substituted stress application (e.g., *so-litary* or *so-lit-tary*).

Phonetically implausible substitutions.   This category included virtually all other miscues that did not result in real words such as omitting syllables or phonemes (e.g., *imagative* for *imaginative*; *judical* for *judicial*), adding syllables or phonemes (e.g., *grugie* for *grudge; heronic* for *heroic*), substituting a phonetically implausible syllable or phoneme (e.g., *permanate* for *permanent; traggady* for *tragedy*). This category also included instances when nonnative speakers substituted complete native language pronunciations for English cognates (e.g., Spanish *ayleeheeblay* for *eligible* or French *trahnkee* for *tranquil*).

Substitutions of real English words.   Any real-word substitution was scored in this category. For example, miscues such as *immorality* for *immortality*, *acquainted* for *acquaintance*, *collaborate* for *celebrate,* and *property* for *prosperity* were all scored in this category.

RESULTS

Descriptive Statistics of Native and Nonnative GE 4 to 6 Groups

Column 1 of Table 1 summarizes results for the 212 ARCS learners enrolled in ABE classes who scored GE 4 to 6 on the DAR Word Recognition subtest. Columns 2 and 3 separate them into native speakers ($n = 135$) and nonnative speakers ($n = 77$); Columns 4 and 5 separate the nonnative speakers into those who learned English before the age of 12 (NNSE < 12; $n = 27$), and those who learned English after 12 (NNSE > 12; $n = 50$). Mean DAR Word Recognition and WRMT–R Word Attack scores do not differ significantly between the native speaker and nonnative speaker groups. As might be expected, the native speakers appear significantly stronger than the nonnative speakers in mean silent reading comprehension (GE 6.60 vs. GE 4.70), $t(210) = 5.56, p < .001$, and mean PPVT–III receptive vocabulary standard scores (80.22 vs. 63.40), $t(210) = 8.77, p < .001$. The patterns of print and comprehension abilities for native and nonnative English speakers address our first two research questions. The native English speakers' comprehension mean of GE 6.60—about 1.5 GE higher than their word-recognition mean—is characteristic of adult readers who have had a history of print skills problems and is consistent with earlier clinical reports (Chall, 1994; Strucker, 1997). Differences are seen in the PPVT–III means between native and nonnative speakers (see previous discussion) and between nonnative speakers who learned English before 12 and those who learned English after 12 ($M = 71.30$ vs. 59.14), $t(75) = 2.90, p < .005$. The native speakers of English are stronger than nonnative speakers of English in oral reading

TABLE 1
Means and Standard Deviations for Print and Comprehension Skills of All GE 4 to 6 and
Subgroups of NSE and NNSE and NNSE < 12 and NNSE > 12

	All GE 4–6[a]	NSE[b]	NNSE[c]	NNSE < 12[d]	NNSE > 12[e]
Print skills					
Word recognition (GE)					
M	4.73	4.78	4.63	4.89	4.50
SD	.72	.75	.65	.64	.62
Word attack raw scores					
M	24.98[f]	24.63[g]	25.60[h]	27.31[i]	24.67[j]
SD	6.68	6.87	6.00	5.10	6.29
Oral reading					
M	6.29	6.62*	5.71	6.80***	5.10
SD	2.42	2.26	2.57	3.01	2.08
Comprehension skills					
Silent reading (GE)					
M	5.92	6.60****	4.70	5.00	4.52
SD	2.59	2.48	2.30	2.30	2.31
PPVT standard scores					
M	74.11	80.22****	63.40	71.30**	59.14
SD	15.65	9.54	18.37	16.54	18.37

Note.   GE = grade equivalent; PPVT = Peabody Picture Vocabulary Test; NSE = native speakers of English; NNSE = nonnative speakers of English; NNSE < 12 = nonnative speakers who learned English before age 12; NNSE > 12 = nonnative speakers who learned English after age 12.
[a]$n = 212.$ [b]$n = 135.$ [c]$n = 77.$ [d]$n = 27.$ [e]$n = 50.$ [f]$n = 207.$ [g]$n = 133.$ [h]$n = 74.$ [i]$n = 26.$ [j]$n = 48.$
*$p < .004.$ **$p < .005.$ ***$p < .01.$ ****$p < .001.$

(mean GE 6.62 vs. GE 5.71), $t(210) = 2.68$, $p < .01$. The nonnative speakers who learned English before age 12 are stronger than the nonnative speakers who learned English after age 12 in oral reading (mean GE 6.80 vs. 5.10), $t(75) = 2.98, p < .004$.

In contrast to the native speakers, nonnative speakers show more even levels of abilities across print and comprehension measures (GE 4.63 on word recognition; GE 4.70 on silent reading comprehension). Their more limited English receptive language ability, as seen in their lower PPVT–III mean scores, probably contributes to their lower achievement in silent reading comprehension (Chall, 1994).

Interestingly, the native speaker and nonnative speaker groups had nearly identical mean raw scores on the WRMT–R Word Attack subtest—usually viewed as a test of pure decoding ability. Clinical experience in the Harvard Adult Reading Laboratory (Chall, 1994; Strucker, 1997) has suggested that native speaker adults at the GE 4–6 level would have had a bit more difficulty with pseudoword tasks than the nonnative speaker adults.

Error Patterns

Based on previous clinical reports (Chall, 1994; Strucker, 1995, 1997) we had expected the GE 4 to 6 NSE to demonstrate stronger achievement than the NNSE on the two meaning-based skills, the PPVT–III and the DAR Silent Reading Comprehension test. But we had not expected to find that the NSE and NNSE did not differ on their mean achievement on Word Attack. To explore this issue, we conducted an error analysis of the decoding abilities of the two groups of GE 4 to 6 learners.

Using the error classification system described previously, we found that native speakers and nonnative speakers showed different patterns of errors, even when their word attack (pseudoword) group means and distributions were virtually identical. T tests for unequal variances were applied to the means of error frequencies for each category of substitution, phonetically plausible, phonetically implausible, and real words. Table 2 shows that native speakers made 2.1 times as many real-word substitutions as compared to the nonnative speakers, whereas the nonnative speakers made 2.7 times as many phonetically plausible errors as the native speakers, $t(88) = 3.99$, $p < .001$ and $t(88) = 3.87$, $p < .001$, respectively.

There was no significant difference in the means of the two language subgroups for substitutions of phonetically implausible words. Nonnative speakers who learned English before age 12 and nonnative speakers who learned English after age 12 did, however, show other differences in their error patterns. Those who learned English after age 12 made 2.3 times as many phonetically plausible substitutions, $t(43) = 3.39$, $p < .002$, as did those who learned English before age 12, and

TABLE 2
Means and Standard Deviations for Types of Word-Recognition Errors: Matched Groups of NSE and NNSE and Subgroups of NNSE (NNSE < 12 and NNSE > 12)

	All NSE[a]	All NNSE[b]	NNSE < 12[c]	NNSE > 12[d]
Phonetically plausible				
M	.40	1.07***	.65	1.5**
SD	.62	.94	.83	.85
Phonetically implausible				
M	3.02	3.84	3.74	3.95
SD	1.23	1.64	1.76	1.52
Real-word substitutions				
M	1.67***	.80	1.17*	.41
SD	1.09	1.04	1.15	.73

Note. NSE = native speakers of English; NNSE = nonnative speakers of English; NNSE < 12 = nonnative speakers who learned English before age 12; NNSE > 12 = nonnative speakers who learned English after age 12.

[a]$n = 45$. [b]$n = 45$. [c]$n = 23$. [d]$n = 22$.

*$p < .01$ (differences between NNSE < 12 and NNSE > 12). **$p < .002$. ***$p < .001$ (differences between NSE and NNSE).

those who learned before age 12 made 2.9 times as many real-word substitutions as did those who learned after age 12, $t(43) = 2.63$, $p < .01$. Thus, in the phonetically plausible and real-word error categories, the nonnative speakers who reported learning English before age 12 occupy a somewhat middle position between the NSE on the one side and the nonnative speakers who learned English after age 12 on the other side.

DISCUSSION

Four research questions guided this inquiry. First, would the pattern of relatively stronger print versus meaning skills in NNSE emerge in the GE 4 to 6 data? Second, would the pattern of relatively stronger meaning versus print skills in NSE emerge in the GE 4 to 6 data? Third, when matched for word recognition and pseudoword decoding, would the patterns of word-recognition errors made by NSE differ from those made by NNSE in the GE 4 to 6 data? And, finally, do the patterns of word-recognition errors of nonnative speakers differ depending on whether their exposure to English took place before or after age 12?

With respect to the first two questions, the patterns Chall (1994) noted were present as relative differences between the two groups but in a slightly different form than Chall described. Specifically, the nonnative speakers had equivalent scores in the print and meaning aspects of reading (word recognition, GE 4.70; silent comprehension, GE 4.70) rather than print skills strength, whereas the native speakers showed greater strength in meaning versus print scores (word recognition, GE 4.73; silent comprehension, GE 6.60). This occurred in our comparison because we held word recognition constant at GE 4 to 6. However, when silent reading comprehension is held constant, the print skills of NSE are significantly lower than nonnative speakers' print skills (Strucker, 1995, 1997; Strucker & Davidson, 2001), as observed by Chall. Another way to express this relation is that the NNSE in ABE classes more resemble normally developing younger readers whose skills are developing evenly in both meaning and print areas, whereas native speakers more resemble children with reading disabilities whose print skills lag behind their meaning skills (Read, 1988a; Read & Ruyter, 1985).

With respect to the third question, NSE made 2.1 times as many real-word substitutions as nonnative speakers, whereas the nonnative speakers made 2.7 times as many phonetically plausible substitutions as the native speakers. Given that both groups had nearly identical raw decoding ability as defined by the pseudoword task, why do they appear to differ on their approaches to reading real words?

The native speakers' preference for real-word substitutions may be rooted in the decoding difficulties that have plagued them since childhood. Similar to what other investigators have reported (Johnson & Blalock, 1987), our clinical work with these GE 4 to 6 readers suggests that some of them have trouble identifying syllable boundaries, especially in the medial and final syllables of long words. Others appear to be able to identify syllable boundaries when specifically asked to do so but fail to apply this knowledge when actually reading.

The mastery/automaticity distinction may play a role in this regard as well. On the pseudoword task, NSE have demonstrated that they can decode when they have no choice, based on their mastery of certain decoding principles. But when reading real words on word-recognition lists, they fall back on their preferred strategy of looking at the first syllable of a word and pronouncing the rest of it based on that first syllable. Perhaps they persist in this strategy because it enables them to read some connected text for comprehension faster than when they attempt to use their slow and unautomatized decoding abilities.

In oral reading of connected text they may be using context to monitor word recognition when their occasional real-word substitutions don't make sense (see Table 1). The GE 4 to 6 native speakers had higher mean scores on the DAR Oral Reading subtest (GE 6.62) and Silent Reading Comprehension (GE 6.60) than on their word recognition (GE 4.78). This difference suggests that like children with reading disabilities, the NSE make use of context to facilitate and confirm word recognition (Chall, 1994; Stanovich, 1986). Their real-word substitution errors may represent attempts to transfer their context-dependent word-recognition strategies to an isolated word-recognition task.

Turning to the NNSE, why do they appear to rely more heavily on decoding than on real-word substitutions? First, as a practical matter, they know the meanings of fewer English words than the native speakers (as shown by PPVT–III comparisons, Table 1), and thus they may have fewer real English words available to substitute. More important, the NNSE resemble normally developing young readers in two respects. First, most of them probably do not have phonologically based reading problems. Strucker (1995) reported that ABE nonnative speakers performed better on a phoneme deletion task in English than ABE NSE. Scholes (1991) reported that adult NNSE whose native languages are alphabetic performed better on phonological awareness tasks than low-literacy adult native speakers, although they performed slightly less well than native English speaking children who were normally developing readers.

Second, as we argued previously, decoding is the preferred approach of normal readers at this stage of reading development (Chall, 1983; Ehri, 1991). When a word is unfamiliar and is not recognized automatically, normal readers decode it because they possess a certain amount of knowledge of how to decode written English. In this connection, some NNSE may be transferring some of the decoding skills (and commitment to using them) that they acquired in their native or first language, provided that theirs was an alphabetic language.

From ARCS we have first language reading data on all native Spanish speakers. Spanish speakers make up 22% of the 75 learners in the GE 4 to 6 nonnative speaker group. Their mean standard score on the Woodcock–Muñoz Batería

Identificación de letras y palabras (word recognition) subtest was 97 ($SD = 26.3$), indicating that their ability to decode Spanish is within the normal range for adults their age. K–12 research suggests (for a review, see Carlo, 2001) that readers who have strong levels of first language decoding are able to transfer that ability to a second or additional language.

It is likely that NNSE approach decoding a new alphabetic language by chunking letter strings into pronounceable syllabic units (i.e., orthographic processing; Adams, 1994; Ehri, 1991). This may be especially true for Spanish speakers whose native language syllable patterns are similar to English. Although this first language/second language orthographic processing transfer is a distinct advantage, it may not be without its problems for first language Spanish speakers. If adult literacy teachers observe that Spanish speakers arrive in class able to break English words into their correct syllables, they may think they can neglect instruction in English phonemes and Spanish/English phoneme contrasts. This in turn could lead students to less accurate reading and perhaps less accurate mapping of oral English onto written English (Parrino, 1998).

With respect to the final question concerning the matched nonnative subgroups, those who learned English before age 12 and those who learned English after age 12 show significant differences in their error patterns (see Table 2). The before-age-12 group showed a similar preference to that of the native English speakers for real-word, as opposed to phonetically plausible, substitutions. When the receptive vocabulary means of the English before-age-12 group are compared to the native speakers, $t(66) = 3.73$, $p < .001$, and to the English after-age-12 group, $t(43) = 2.25$, $p < .03$, they appear to occupy a distinct middle position (see Table 3). However, their word-recognition mean is not significantly different from either group.

Examination of ARCS questionnaire data for the group of nonnative speakers who learned English before age 12 reveals that 48% reported receiving early help in English reading in the form of Chapter 1, special education placement, or both, suggesting that some of them had early reading difficulties with English that were recognized by their teachers in the United States. Whether those difficulties were the result of reading disability or simply second-language literacy acquisition problems (or both) cannot be determined from these data. Similar to the native speakers at the GE 4 to 6 level in ABE, many of these participants had exposure to English reading instruction but came away from it with limited reading skills.

Thus, taken together with their educational histories, the error patterns of the nonnative speakers who learned English before age 12 indicate that they may have similar decoding and fluency difficulties that are present among the native speakers.

Implications for Research

The purpose of the ARCS was to describe the reading of a large sample of adult literacy learners in ways that would be useful to policymakers, practitioners, and cur-

TABLE 3
Means and Standard Deviations for PPVT–III and Word Recognition
for Matched Sample: NSE, NNSE < 12, and NNSE > 12

		NNSE	
	NSE^a	$< 12^b$	$>12^c$
PPVT			
M	80.28**	68.26*	55.73
SD	8.20	18.45	18.92
DAR word recognition			
M	4.79	4.76	4.50
SD	.75	.63	.60

Note. PPVT = Peabody Picture Vocabulary Test; NSE = native speakes of English; NNSE = nonnative speakers of English. NNSE < 12 = nonnative speakers who learned English before age 12; NNSE > 12 = nonnative speakers who learned English after age 12; DAR = Diagnostic Assessments of Reading.
$^a n = 45.$ $^b n = 23.$ $^c n = 22.$
*p < .03 NNSE < 12 compared to NNSE > 12. **p < .001 NSE compared to NNSE < 12.

riculum designers. The comparisons presented in this article are based on secondary analyses of these descriptive data. First, we consider possible alternative interpretations of these results, and, second, we raise questions that should be addressed in future research.

Could the differences we observed between NSE and NNSE error patterns be influenced by the types of words that appeared on the DAR GE 5, 6, and 7 Word Recognition lists (the highest levels read by readers in the GE 4 to 6 range)? For example, if those lists had included many nonphonetic words, this might have led both native speakers and nonnative speakers to make more nonphonetic errors, perhaps exaggerating a tendency on the part of the native speakers to make real-word substitutions. Examination of the 30 words (see Appendix) shows the opposite: Only 1 word out of 30 (*fierce*) could be classified as not phonetically regular, whereas the remaining 29 words lend themselves to the direct application of English phonics rules. Therefore, it could be argued that those 29 words presented a similar challenge to both groups, a challenge that involved using similar phonics principles to those they used on the pseudoword task. Subsequent research using word lists containing both phonetically regular and nonphonetic words would help to resolve this issue.

We also wonder whether our categories for classifying errors might have influenced the results. Although the real-word substitution category is straightforward, we note that our phonetically plausible category was very strict in that all syllables and phonemes had to be present, and only plausible changes in stress and vowel pronunciation were allowable in this category. Most errors (59.57% of the NSE and

65.33% of the NNSE) were classified in the not phonetically plausible category. A more fine-grained classification system that tracked partially correct or partially plausible errors might prove useful in further understanding the apparent differences in the decoding strategies of NSE and NNSE. Because adults with reading disabilities frequently decode the initial syllables of polysyllabic words correctly, then go on to make errors on the medial or final syllables (Johnson & Blalock, 1987; Strucker, 1995), it would be important to know whether those kinds of partial errors are made with similar or differential frequency by the NSE and NNSE.

Another useful question to explore is whether the NSE and NNSE error patterns we observed in word recognition would also emerge in the oral reading of connected text. Such research might also provide a better window into what word-recognition strategies the two groups might be using in silent reading.

Implications for Instruction

We turn now to the state of instruction in adult literacy centers and what these results might imply for their current practices. Many adult literacy centers place students in classes using a single silent reading comprehension score (for a lengthier discussion of this topic see Strucker, 1995, 1997). Based on that single score, native speakers, many of whom need work in the print aspects of reading, are often placed in the same class with nonnative speakers whose decoding may be several GEs higher. Teachers come to realize this over time. But at best this means that they have to divide their scant instructional hours, using half the time to teach decoding to the native speakers that the nonnative speakers have already mastered and using the other half of the time to teach vocabulary to the nonnative speakers that the native speakers already know. Where possible, adult literacy centers should consider offering separate classes to accommodate the needs of these two different kinds of readers. To identify these needs they will need to assess word-recognition and vocabulary, not just silent reading comprehension.

Normally developing K–3 readers are thought to progress from sounding out phoneme–grapheme correspondences to the ability to recognize permissible syllable patterns (Adams, 1994; Chall, 1983; Ehri, 1991), moving from basic decoding to fluency. Perhaps the GE 4 to 6 adult NSE have stalled despite having basic decoding knowledge and have made an incomplete transition to the orthographic processing of syllable patterns. Although the native speakers' performance on the PPVT–III was stronger than that of the nonnative speakers (Table 1), the native speakers are, nevertheless, only at the 10th percentile of the norming population. Given this absolute weakness in receptive vocabulary and their reported childhood reading difficulties, the preference of the native speakers for real-word substitutions may be an inefficient strategy for long-term growth in reading. One can only substitute real words one has heard or already mastered, so one's vocabulary places an uppermost limit on the substitutions that can be made. And, it is likely that these learners will need to read in content areas (as opposed to relying on oral encounters) to acquire more advanced vocabulary (Chall, 1987). The GE 4 to 6 NSE may be relying on a meaning-driven decoding strategy (i.e., their limited knowledge of English words) that directs them away from the analysis, mastery, and overlearning of the lower frequency syllable patterns. Yet they will need this independent decoding ability to "read to learn" (Chall, 1983, 1987) when they encounter more challenging and less familiar material.

Whatever the reasons for this limiting decoding strategy among GE 4 to 6 NSE, the instructional implications for adult literacy teachers are straightforward. Although these learners appear to have partial knowledge of the phonics and syllable patterns that they will need to make further progress, they must be encouraged to practice them to the point of automaticity and to learn any new patterns they do not know. Moreover, they must be won over to the strategy of using those decoding patterns consistently when reading connected text.

The NNSE appear more committed to a phonetic decoding strategy, and in this sense they resemble normally developing younger readers at the GE 4 to 6 level. But at this level they too will begin to encounter less familiar phonics patterns and unusual pronunciations. Some less familiar pronunciations such as *ch* pronounced as /k/ in many scientific words (e.g., *synchronize*) and unusual stress patterns (e.g., *monotony*) are learned when those words are learned in school subjects. A phonetically plausible error, such as *adaquait* for *adequate,* might be related to lack of English vocabulary and syntactic knowledge. English often uses the long *a* pronunciation of final syllable *–ate* when the word is a verb and the schwa pronunciation of *–ate* when the word is an adjective.

Teachers should be aware that the NNSE < 12, like the native speakers, could be helped by the overlearning of phonics principles and syllable patterns and oral reading practice to improve fluency. And, like the latter group, they need to be committed to employing this strategy.

For the nonnative speakers, English morphosyntactic information and vocabulary should be part of decoding instruction, especially as they, like the NSE, begin to encounter written English that differs significantly from the familiar and conversational (Chafe & Danielwicz, 1987; Chall, 1983, 1987).

Finally, the results presented suggest that highly similar achievement scores on a task such as the WRMT–R Word Attack test do not necessarily mean that all students within that scoring range use similar decoding strategies for real words. Some may be more committed to phonetic decoding than others. To design effective instruction, teachers who work with GE 4 to 6 adults need to know not only what phonics principles their students appear to have mastered but also what phonics principles they actually use with automaticity when they read.

ACKNOWLEDGMENTS

The ARCS was funded by the U.S. Department of Education, Office of Educational Research and Improvement, and the Office of Vocational and Adult Education. We acknowledge the assistance of Kelly Bruce in scoring and coding the ARCS assessments and in categorizing the word-recognition errors for this analysis.

REFERENCES

Adams, M. J. (1994). *Beginning to read: Thinking and learning about print.* Cambridge, MA: MIT Press.

Bruck, M. (1990). Word-recognition skills of adults with childhood diagnoses of dyslexia. *Developmental Psychology, 26,* 439–454.

Bruck, M. (1992). Persistence of dyslexic's phonological awareness deficits. *Developmental Psychology, 28,* 874–886.

Carlo, M. S. (2001). *Do reading skills transfer across languages? Examining the literature from a component process perspective on reading* (Office of Bilingual Education and Minority Language Affairs Report). Washington, DC: U.S. Office of Education.

Chafe, W., & Danielwicz, J. (1987). *Properties of spoken and written language* (Tech. Rep. No. 5). Berkeley: University of California, Center for the Study of Writing.

Chall, J. S. (1983). *Stages of reading development.* New York: McGraw-Hill.

Chall, J. S. (1987). Developing literacy in children and adults. In D. Wagner (Ed.), *The future of literacy in a changing world* (pp. 65–80). New York: Pergamon.

Chall, J. S. (1994). Patterns of adult reading. *Learning Disabilities, 5,* 29–33.

Dunn, L. M., Dunn, L. M., & Dunn, D. M. (1997). *Peabody Picture Vocabulary Test III (PPVT–III).* Circle Pines, MN: American Guidance Service.

Ehri, L. C. (1991). Development of the ability to read words. In R. Barr, M. Kamil, P. Mosenthal, & P. D. Pearson (Eds.), *Handbook of reading research* (Vol. 2, pp. 383–417). New York: Longman.

Fink, R. P. (1998). Literacy development in successful men and women with dyslexia. *Annals of Dyslexia, 48,* 311–342.

Greenberg, D., Ehri, L. C., & Perin, D. (1997). Are word reading processes the same or different in adult literacy students and third–fifth graders matched for reading level? *Journal of Educational Psychology, 89,* 262–275.

Greenberg, D., Ehri, L. C., & Perin, D. (2002). Do adult literacy students make the same word-reading and spelling errors as children matched for word-reading age? *Scientific Studies of Reading, 6,* 245–265.

Johnson, D. J., & Blalock, J. W. (1987). *Adults with learning disabilities.* New York: Harcourt-Brace.

Parrino, A. (1998). The politics of pronunciation and the adult learner. In T. Smoke (Ed.), *Adult ESL* (pp. 171–184). Mahwah, NJ: Lawrence Elrbaum Associates, Inc.

Pratt, A. C., & Brady, S. (1988). Relation of phonological awareness to reading disability in children and adults. *Journal of Educational Psychology, 80,* 319–323.

Read, C. (1988a). *Adults who read like children: The psycholinguistic bases* (Final report to the U.S. Department of Education). Madison: University of Wisconsin, Center for Education Research.

Read, C. (1988b). *Phonological awareness and adult readers* (Final report to the U.S. Department of Education). Madison: University of Wisconsin, Center for Education Research.

Read, C., & Ruyter, L. (1985). Reading and spelling skills in adults of low literacy. *Remedial and Special Eduction, 6,* 43–52.

Rosner, J. (1975). *Helping children overcome learning difficulties.* New York: Walker.

Roswell, F. G., & Chall, J. S. (1992). *Diagnostic Assessments of Reading (DAR).* Itaska, IL: Riverside.

Sabatini, J. (2002). Efficiency in word reading of adults: Ability group comparisons. *Scientific Studies of Reading, 6,* 267–298.

Scholes, R. J. (1991). Phoneme deletion and literacy in native and non-native speakers of English. *Journal of Research in Reading, 14,* 130–140.

Shafir, U., & Siegel, L. S. (1994). Subtypes of learning disabilities in adolescents and adults. *Journal of Learning Disabilities, 27,* 123–134.

Snow, C., & Strucker, J. (2000). Lessons from *Preventing reading difficulties in young children* for adult learning and literacy. In J. Comings, B. Garner, & C. Smith (Eds.), *Annual review of adult learning and literacy* (Vol. 1, pp. 25–73). San Francisco: Jossey-Bass.

Spreen, O., & Haaf, R. G. (1986). Empirically derived learning disability subtypes: A replication attempt and longitudinal patterns over 15 years. *Journal of Learning Disabilities, 19,* 170–180.

Stanovich, K. E. (1986). Matthew effects in reading: Some consequences of individual differences in the acquisition of literacy. *Reading Research Quarterly, 21,* 360–406.

Strucker, J. (1995). *Patterns of reading in adult education.* Unpublished doctoral dissertation, Harvard University, Cambridge, MA.

Strucker, J. (1997). *The reading component approach.* Monograph prepared for the Massachusetts Bureau of Adult Education System. Cambridge, MA: National Center for the Study of Adult Learning and Literacy.

Strucker, J., & Davidson, R. (2002). *National Center for the Study of Adult Learning and Literacy report.* Manuscript in preparation.

Strucker, J., & Davidson, R., & Reddy, L. (1998). *Adult Reading Components Study examiners' manual.* Unpublished manuscript, National Center for the Study of Adult Learning and Literacy, Cambridge, MA.

Wechsler, D. (1997). *Wechsler Adult Intelligence Scale–III.* San Antonio, TX: The Psychological Corporation.

Wolf, M. (1991). Naming speed and reading: The contribution of the cognitive neurosciences. *Reading Research Quarterly, 26*(2), 123–141.

Woodcock, R. W. (1987). *Woodcock Reading Mastery Test–Revised (WRMT–R).* Circle Pines, MN: American Guidance Service.

Woodcock, R. W., & Muñoz, A. F. (1996). *Batería Woodcock-Muñoz.* Itaska, IL: Riverside.

Manuscript received August 2, 2001
Final revision received December 4, 2001
Accepted December 5, 2001

APPENDIX
Target Words, Word-Recognition Lists, Levels 5–7, and Real-Word Substitutions

Target Word	Substitution(s)
Acquaintance	Accusation; Acquaint; Acquainted
Adequate	
Affectionate	Affection
Ancestor	Ancestors; Announcer
Association	
Competitor	
Concentration	Concentrate; Consideration; Construction
Conservative	Conservation; Conversation
Eligible	Eligibility; Illegible; Legible
Emphasis	Emphasize
Enthusiastic	
Excursion	Execution; Incursion
Exhaust	Exhausted
Extinct	Exciting; Exhibit; Exist; Extension; Extent; Instinct
Fierce	Fence; Fiancé; Fire; First; Fleece; Force; Friends; Furious; Furnace
Grudge	Grunge
Heroic	Erotic; Heretic; Hero
Humiliate	Humiliated; Humility
Imaginative	Emanation; Imagination
Immediate	Imaginative; Imitate; Immediately; Immigrate; Immunity
Immortality	Immorality; Immorally; Mortality
Ingenious	Genius; Ingenuous
Maintenance	
Obedient	
Particular	Parasol; Partial; Particle; Particles; Particularly; Practical
Precaution	Precautions; Precision
Prosperity	
Readjustment	
Solitary	Solidarity; Solitaire
Supremacy	